Anke Schwörer-Haag
Thomas Haag

Dream Team

Anke Schwörer-Haag • Thomas Haag

Dream Team
Riding in Harmony
Schooling of the Icelandic Horse

Published by:
Birgit Nonnenprediger

With 24 black and white photos
From Ueli Heller (p.15 and 99 top), Günther Hess (p.95), Eirikur Jönsson (p.150), Anke Schwörer-Haag (p.37 (3), 50, 79, 81, 100, 101, 115). From the Schwörer's archive (p.7, 11, 12, 13, 16, 41, 74 (2), 77, 99 bottom, 108) and 58 drawings from Elisabeth German.

Cover Design: Birgit Nonnenprediger,
use of a coloured photo from André Welle.
Translation: Rita Austin
Revision: Fi Pugh
Proof-reading: Pamela Turner, James Joicy
Production: Birgit Nonnenprediger
Sales & Marketing: Birgit Nonnenprediger
The Stables, Copsley Court
Gayhouse Lane, Outwood
Surrey RH1 5PP, United Kingdom
Web site: www.dream-teams.com

© 1991 Franckh-Kosmos Verlags GMBH & CO.
Original title: Gaedingar - Die andere Reitlehre
Islandpferde besser reiten

ISBN 0 9536425 0 X
Printed in England
Typesetting: Elite Typesetting Techniques, Hampshire
Printing & Binding: MPG BOOKS LTD, Cornwall

Publisher's Note

I have found the Icelandic horse fascinating ever since I saw and rode one for the first time.
I am sure many of you feel the same.

Although I live in England, I have had the advantage of being able to read books about them in German. And there are many. My favourite book has always been "Gaedingar". Since I had difficulty sharing my experience with my horse friends, I decided to find a way of producing this title in English. Well, here it is.

I would like to thank my partner Frank for his support and motivation throughout the whole project. Special thanks to Rita who did a great job with the translation and to Fi for her careful revision of the book. Thanks also to proof-readers Pamela Turner and James Joicey as well as to the authors Anke Schwörer-Haag and Thomas Haag and the German publishing company Franckh-Kosmos Verlag.

I hope that you enjoy reading this book in your language as much as I enjoyed it reading it for the first time in German. Although it is my mother tongue I had to read it a couple of times before I really understood the whole content. So don't worry if the same happens to you.

I am well on the way to becoming a Dream Team with my horse "Lyftingur". I hope you will be able to say the same soon.

Birgit

CONTENTS

Introduction   1

The origins: functional riding   3
A brief synopsis of the history of Icelandic Horse riding with an amazing conclusion: there is a way to have a dream horse of your own, a technique that is tailored to the needs of many leisure and competition riders and their horses, enabling even the less talented, whether two or four legged, to become a dream team.

Training the rider   11
The position of the rider   11
How to give aids without being forced into the 'correct position', yet remaining in harmony.
The aids   12
The horse learns a foreign language. Its movements are the basis for creating the rider's position.
The legs   13
A supple horse will accept the rider's leg aids. Any forceful use of leg aids to drive a horse forward is pointless.
The seat   15
Only when the rider is able to employ a swivel seat does he take advantage of all the possibilities that the influence of weight provides.
The back   17
This is seen as the key position for harmony between horse and rider, as a rider cannot use his back effectively when the horse is tense and favours the lateral.
The hands   20
This chapter explains why a rather antiquated custom in teaching the rider, namely the command 'Keep your hands still', should be abolished. Classical riding instructors never actually said this, nor did they mean it in this way.
The combined use of the aids   23
The half halt is the foundation for harmony between horse and rider. As with many basic exercises a great number of riders think they can use it correctly after a short while. Only with ongoing training do they recognise how subtle an influence is needed to execute a half halt. The most difficult part is the second phase, where the horse should reach out for the giving reins and rebalance in the shortest of time. More advanced versions of the half halt are the halt and the rein back.
Basic exercises   28
The basic vocabulary for the conversation between rider and horse consists of exercises like moving-off, riding of turns, leg yielding and turns on the forehand and on the haunches. Why they have to be ridden exactly as described, and mistakes that should be avoided.

Training the horse 33
We talk about the time one should take for training, why the relationship between rider and horse is so important and the role the terrain can play when riding.
Groundwork 35
Leading, lungeing, loose schooling and hand horse training can be seen as the ABC. The trainer, with skill and patience, can make things easier for himself and for the horse, by building a foundation on which to base further schooling.
Starting the young horse 43
Backing successfully and without confrontation. How to teach the basic vocabulary of a 'foreign language' to the horse: leg aids, half halts, turning, leg yielding, turns on the forehand, half pirouettes and rein back.

Natural crookedness 49
Why the horse has a stiff and a soft side. Why it's no good to try to work on the stiff side and why a harmonious relationship has to be re-established every time the rider mounts .

Self-carriage of the horse 53
Where the beautiful or ugly outline of a horse is created. Why one shouldn't concentrate on head, neck and forelegs, but look at quarters, back and shoulders first. What self-carriage has to do with positive or negative flow, and why it is especially harsh for a horse to be forced into a dressage-like outline.

Gaits 58
This chapter does away with the old belief in five, clearly divided gaits of the Icelandic Horse. It explains why it is important for training, as well as for the fun element in riding, to look upon the gaits as the ability of the horse to change fluently between lateral and diagonal movements. It clarifies why tense horses don't provide a comfortable ride and how one can address this problem by playing with the gaits, and take advantage of the horse's natural talents. It also gives you an idea what the expression 'on the bit' really means and why it is deceitful to manipulate the horse's action artificially.
Training for the different gaits 67
How different types of horse can progress, based on their individual talents. How careful selection of riding terrain and the use of the 'gait map' can be advantageous.
Walk 70
Most Icelandic Horses have a good walk. Why problems in walk can be a sign of faults in overall training.
Trot 71
Why gaited horses that prefer to trot in a clear two-beat can still be stiff and how to help them.
Tölt 74
Exercises that suit a supple tölter and problems that can arise during training. How to train a pacey tölter and bring him towards a clear four-beat. How to teach tölt to horses that are stiff and trotty and how to balance a horse that is stiff and pacey. How to

teach a horse the different tempi in tölt and faults that must be avoided.

Canter **87**

Why a clear three-beat canter is not favoured at first and how to use canter to relax a horse.

Flying pace **92**

How to school and train different types of flying pacers. How to ride a pace race and mistakes that should be avoided when actually riding pace, as well as when 'switching' or 'checking' the pacing horse.

Competition riding **102**

Some basic comments on competition riding and how to incorporate them into the horse's training.

Saddlery and tack **104**

The requirements of a saddle and what we think about some specialist saddles. Which bits work well. When and why the horse's legs need special protection.

Introduction

Gæðingur – a horse that shows all gaits with grace and harmony.

Gæðingur – a ladies' mount, a comfortable and pleasurable ride – plus an elegant and impressive looking horse.

Gæðingur – this is the word the Icelanders have given to their 'dream horse' – a horse that is the desire of every Icelandic Horse rider

who has ever had the privilege to see one, or – for a magical moment – has been allowed to ride one.

They are rare, these dream horses, where even the novice immediately recognises that there is 'something special' in their extraordinary performance. These 'superstars' are few and far between, mastering the most difficult of tasks with the greatest of ease, always proud and self-confident.

Their performance is unforgettable, no matter what the discipline – be it the Icelandic Horse *Rödull*,

The epitome of a Gæðingur: German, European and World Champion Bernd Vith riding Rödull von Ellenbach. Rider and horse in total harmony.

ridden by Bernd Vith, in a class of his own as German and European Champion, or *Milton* the show-jumping sensation, who conquered the most difficult courses, apparently jumping by himself.

Unfortunately, these four-legged 'dancers' can be counted on the fingers of one hand. Their movements flow through their whole bodies, they change gaits or tempi so lightly and easily that not only the rider but also the spectator has an unforgettable experience.

But far too often we see spectacular horses, but so rigid in the back that the rider can't go with the movement. At many shows, horses are presented close to boiling point and fighting for the bit. These are horses who have the physical ability to perform well, but are let down by their tense, crude and clumsy action.

It is common to see horses whose faces show that they are unhappy and stressed. Rolling eyes and flattened ears leave no doubt whatsoever that they do not enjoy their work. These horses are light-years away from the *Gæðingur*. Their riders force them into a constant battle and one can see, as soon as gait or tempo is changed, that they are looking forward to the end of the riding session.

But this is not just confined to shows. On pleasure rides and similar leisure activities, one can see many riders locked in combat with their horses, for hours or even days. Instead of relaxing and just enjoying being together, appreciating nature, beautiful bridleways and glorious weather, the two partners, horse and rider, are so out of tune with each other, that the whole experience ends in pure stress.

This is where this book comes in. All riders who agree with us in thinking: "It doesn't have to be that way", should find some food for thought in the following pages, sparking discussions on the way.

We are claiming, right at the beginning, that every horse can come closer to the ideal of the 'dream horse' – the *Gæðingur*, or whatever other riding nations may call their ideal horse. We are convinced that every horse, with the appropriate training, can give a pleasurable and smooth ride.

The real 'dream horses' will succeed more quickly – almost of their own accord, because Mother Nature has equipped them with the necessary abilities. Others might take longer, because inherent shortfalls have to be put right. It is our experience that the less talented a horse is, the better the character and temperament must be. They will need greater willingness to co-operate in order to achieve the same goals as their talented counterparts.

We honestly believe that every rider – if he tries hard enough – can grow together with his horse to form a 'dream team'. Both will then be able to experience 'the magic', no matter what adventure they have planned: a gentle hack, a trail through unspoiled countryside, a local show or an important competition.

As riding Icelandic Horses is still a relatively new activity, the coming years will see a lot of development in the riding of Icelandic Horses, both for leisure and competition riders.

But all such development in riding will be in the right direction if the ultimate goal remains the 'dream horse'. Achieving this goal can be made faster, better and easier for the horse, but one should never lose sight of the ultimate ambition: the *Gæðingur*.

The Origins: Functional Riding

In days gone by, riding purely and simply served the sole purpose of getting from one place to another more quickly. Every traveller had to use a riding animal of some sort, be it a horse, donkey or another beast of burden. In areas not served by roads, this remained necessary into the twentieth century. Iceland was no exception. There, as everywhere else, a sort of functional riding was 'cultivated'. The riding position resulted from a compromise between the many requirements to which the riders subjected their horses. Only in the rarest cases was a specific gait or a dressage movement performed.

The Seat: Proud and Comfortable

Riders in Iceland sat comfortably in the saddle: they kept their upper body proudly upright, leaning back slightly, legs braced forward against the stirrups and holding their hands relatively high. For a bridle they used the Icelandic curb bit, usually with heavy, loose reins. It was the sheer weight of the cheeks, combined with heavy reins, that encouraged better self carriage of the horse and formed the beautiful images of proud Icelandic Horses that we all remember.

Icelanders used a saddle with short flaps, because their lower legs did not touch the horse. The use of a crupper was common, as this helped to fix the saddle in rough terrain. This was also necessary because horses were not yet bred for riding and the withers were often not very high.

Horses were not required to perform specific gaits, but most riders selected a horse that was naturally forward going and allowed it to cover long distances in the gait it happened to prefer. For this reason, horses with smooth, supple movements were prized and much

Icelandic farmers sat rather upright, proud and comfortable in the saddle. They always selected the nicest riding horses for themselves and their families.

sought after. Hard and uncomfortable horses were, if possible, avoided. Icelandic farmers used their horses for work and were rarely interested in giving special training to untalented horses. As riding was primarily a means to an end, mostly covering long distances over rough country, a style of riding evolved which was best suited to these conditions.

The Beginnings of the Search for Style

In the middle of the 20th century things changed. Riding was no longer merely a means of transportation. It became an end in itself. In Iceland, there was increased activity in the breeding of riding horses and with it came the export trade. Continental Europeans got to know about tölt and flying pace and Icelanders were brought face to face with the disciplines of dressage and show-jumping. This led to mutual influencing of riding styles. For example, Icelanders began to try rising trot, which they had previously never found necessary. Because their horses didn't have the same strong back movements of the larger Warmbloods, the rider was hardly thrown out of the saddle of a trotting Icelandic Horse; therefore posting was virtually unknown up to that time.

Riders on the Continent, on the other hand, found themselves in completely uncharted territory with the tölt and pace gaits. Nobody knew how these gaits were supposed to be ridden. Riders therefore copied some parts of the riding style from the country where the breed originated and combined them, more or less successfully, with the way of riding that was conventional in their own country.

Standards soon improved. After they had unlocked the 'secret' of tölt and pace, leisure riders, competition riders and trainers alike developed the best methods for riding and improving these gaits. But the search for the most appropriate riding style continued.

The gaits of tölt and flying pace were a complete novelty for riders on the European Continent. They therefore copied some aspects of the Icelandic riding style and combined them, more or less successfully, with the conventional way of riding in their own country.

The search for style

Landsmót Tölt Champion 1978: Hlynur frá Akureyri ridden by Eyjólfur Ísólfsson

Other influences
At the beginning of the 1970s, a few riders of Icelandic Horses made contact with American gaited horse trainers. The American influence signalled the beginning of manipulating the action of the Icelandic Horse by means of weight on the horses' legs. These experiments reached their climax at the European Championships in 1979 in Uddel, at which some horses were re-shod several times between tests. This resulted in a complete ban on weight manipulation, not least on grounds of animal welfare, and re-shoeing during a competition was prohibited.

In the search for a viable method of training, other riders tried to school their horses according to the principles of "classical" horsemanship. They also failed.

Because they misunderstood the intentions of the classical masters, they restricted themselves and their horses to grinding away at lessons in the 'sandpit', using side reins or similar aids to impose a 'dressage type' carriage. However, because tölt and pace were not logically included in the initial concept, and the rules of

A partnership that dominated the scene and remained unchallenged for years: Christiane Matthiesen and Gammur frá Hofsstöðum.

classical riding were not followed through from basic principles (which state: "encourage the natural movement of the horse and never ask for anything which does not occur naturally") the achieved outline was not the result of exercising the whole body. These horses actually looked quite good in walk, trot and canter, but their performance in tölt and pace was poor.

The result of these experiments with riding styles was often frustrating. In many cases they were a harsh experience for the horse. The fact that they co-operated at all is testimony to the readiness of this breed to perform and to its rider-friendly disposition.

But it wasn't all doom and gloom. There were horses that had the ability to send even the most critical spectators into raptures. Horses such as *Hlynur frá Akureyri* (Landsmót Tölt Champion 1978), *Gammur frá Hofsstöðum* (multiple European Tölt Champion), *Muni frá Ketilsstöðum* (Landsmót Champion 1990, with a 10 mark for tölt), *Brjánn frá Hólum* (World Tölt Champion 1987 in Weißtrach), *Rödull von Ellenbach*

(German and World Champion Tölt 1989) or *Gilfi vom Ponsheimer Hof*, all proved that a supple tölter allows its rider to remain seated in the saddle at all times. They all strengthen our belief that total harmony between horse and rider need not be restricted to a simple hack or a novice performance, but can be extended to top class performances as well.

There must therefore be ways to achieve this goal. Irrespective of which rider we observed on these light and easily moving horses they all sat deep and relaxed, allowing themselves to be carried along by the movement. Their tactful and gentle aids could have come straight out of a textbook. The more deeply we researched, the more convinced we became that there is no point in mixing various styles of riding or using them for the wrong purpose.

Anyone who decides to ride the Icelandic way must learn to think like the Icelanders. There, as it happens, it is frowned upon to invest a great deal of time in an untalented horse. Due to many years of excellent breeding, riders have such a wide choice that they only have to concern themselves with the very best horses. Iceland's wide, open spaces allow riders to incorporate the fiery temperament and great will of these horses into their training. There the riders can let their horses go and devote time and attention to the various characters and abilities, thus finding harmony.

Those who prefer the American show style, and who want to reach their goal with weights and other artificial aids, must examine both closely and honestly the result of this type of training. They must also accept that these horses may end up facing a dock operation and will constantly have to wear sweat packs in order to change from the degraded creatures they are into seemingly self confident animals with fine necks and proudly carried tails.

We believe there is another way. We want to use this book to present ideas and give something to think about, to find a style that suits as many horses and riders as possible. We want to show a way by which perhaps even less gifted horses and humans have a chance of becoming a 'dream team'. The result we are aiming for is captured in the words

The whole of Iceland was cheering when Sigurbjörn (Diddi) Bárðarson and Brjánn frá Hólum became Tölt World Champions. Diddi later coined the phrase: "Riding is a dance between two friends".

Reynir Aðalsteinsson has been presenting Icelandic Horses with great success, skill and extreme sensitivity for decades. He has participated in almost every European Championship and countless big shows – appearing on the winners' list most of the time. Here he partners Sproti frá Torfastöðum at the 1983 European Championship in Roderath, securing a third place in the five-gait, second in the pace race (22.0 seconds) and second in the pace test.

The search for style 9

of Sigurbjörn Bárðarson, after his World Championship victory with *Brjánn frá Hólum*. He said: "riding is a dance between two friends". Whether our ideas really do get to the heart of the matter, only time will tell. It is, however, to be hoped that they will inspire every rider, no matter what stage of training he has reached, to think about or discuss the subject. If we have succeeded, the rider might even read this book more than once, discovering as he does so, more and more arguments that initially seemed unimportant to him. We believe that it is worthwhile to think this method through to its logical conclusion.

Spectacular action and still a relaxed seat: Andrea Jänisch and Gilfi vom Ponsheimer Hof.

Training the Rider

The Position of the Rider

Time and again, in riding courses and lessons, we come across detailed descriptions of the 'correct classical position'. With plumb line, tape measure and ruler, measurable and assessable criteria are set in stone. We think this is wrong. It is true, when we talk about aids later on, that certain sitting positions have their justification, since they permit refined, direct and sympathetic aids. The start of a rider's training however, is no place for demanding the correct position. If the beginner is forced into a rigid system, it will only lead to excessive tension and stiffness, never to a good, harmonious 'conversation' with the horse.

The first goal in the rider's training is therefore to achieve a smooth, well balanced seat with weight evenly distributed on both seat bones – the basic seat. However, it often takes a long time before the rider is able to sit relaxed in all situations.

To begin with, all of the beginner's efforts will be directed towards merely staying on. Until he has developed a feeling of balance in all gaits and tempi, the rider will always be tempted to hold on tight, with his thighs, knees, lower legs and hands. This 'gripping' leads to excessive tension. It is therefore the instructor's first task to break down this tension and improve the rider's suppleness.

The rider learns to sit

This is best achieved on the lunge, using an experienced and well-trained horse that is not unsettled by a beginner's awkwardness nor put off its stride. Only by concentrating on himself can the rider achieve relaxation, helped by the following mounted exercises: steady circling of the arms, special breathing exercises or riding without stirrups. Exercising in a relaxed atmosphere is generally very helpful.

In conversation with the instructor, a pupil will learn which feelings he should experience and he can clearly judge the stage he has reached in his training by constantly relating what he feels.

If the instructor wants to get the beginner into a position from which the pupil can best influence the movements of the horse, he will get him to practise the various aids over and over again, pointing out positive or negative reactions as they go along. The rider's suppleness and sense of balance will increase as he learns to go with the movements of his horse. Riding out or jumping exercises are just as

This horse is letting the rider sit. The movement comes from its hindquarters, like a wave or a flowing river, through the spine of the horse to its mouth. The 'conversation' between horse and rider, based on a language of harmony, is working well.

A totally different picture where the horse is tense: the movement from the quarters is blocked at the back and the shoulder remains low. The rider can hardly sit, as there seems to be a hole in front of the saddle. The horse doesn't slope uphill.

good for relaxation as lessons on the lunge. At every stage of his training, the rider is advised to go back to these exercises in order to prevent or, if necessary, eliminate any stiffness.

The Aids

The language the rider uses for communicating with the horse is called: 'Aids'. The art of riding ultimately consists of using the right aid, in the appropriate dosage, at the correct point in time (this also sums up a 'tactful rider'). In the figurative sense, the training of a horse – which converses with its own kind in its mother tongue – can be compared to the learning of a foreign language. The animal must learn to observe and to interpret the rider's commands, body language and aids. During his training, the rider himself must learn the logically structured and universally recognised language of the aids, in order to be able to communicate with any horse trained by this method.

Because all movement comes from the hindquarters, this system is constructed from back to front. Leg aids produce movement from the haunches. The seat transports this movement, like a wave or a flowing river, through the spine of the horse to its mouth, where the hands pick up the wave and make it flow back.

Mutual Influence

This movement, based on the image of a wave, can be influenced by the rider in a positive or negative way: the more flexible his seat, the more sympathetic his aids, the better the horse accepts the flow of the wave movement. The rider, after all, is sitting in the centre of this movement and the more refined his aids, the better the horse will respond.

If a tense rider simply bounces up and down on a horse's back, he is interrupting this wave movement. As a result, the horse becomes tense and the rider has even less chance of sitting properly. He will bounce even more, his hands will become stiff and hard – and so will the horse. Things will get worse and worse...

This process may be described as the phenomenon of mutual influence: the horse's movements influence the rider's seat (see also the section on Back Aids), whilst on the other hand the rider's seat influences the horse.

Let us now turn to the ways in which the rider can convey his wishes to the horse.

The Legs

When riders talk about leg aids they usually mean the use of the lower leg. At the beginning of training, the rider casually lays his calves against the horse's sides. At this stage it is almost impossible to purposefully move the horse on, and later on it will be successful only in a few situations. Therefore, the rider uses his lower legs just to keep contact. The more the horse relaxes, the more

The rider's leg on the girth (left) encourages the hindleg on the same side to swing further forward, or it drives the horse sideways. The rider's leg, about a hand span behind the girth (right), contains the movement, i.e. it stops the 'falling out' of the hindleg on the same side when riding circles, or driving laterally - for instance when turning on the haunches.

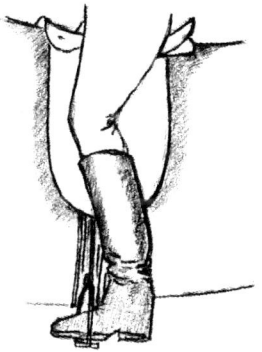
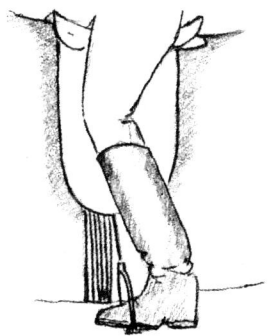

distinctly the even swing of the body creates a right-left rhythm for a light encouraging leg to follow. Application on one side will encourage the horse to move the hindleg on that side forward. Any forceful use of leg aids, to drive the horse forward, is pointless.

The better trained a horse is, the more sensitively it will react to leg aids. As a matter of principle, the rider should never attempt to drive a lethargic horse forward by heavy thumping or even kicking with his legs. The voice, the appropriate use of a riding crop, or a lead horse will render significantly better service in these circumstances.

Positions and functions of the lower legs

The four major influences of the legs depend on different combinations of use and position:

-To create forward movement, slight pressure with the leg on the girth encourages the hindleg on the same side to swing further forward.

-Prevent the hindquarters falling out, by placing the leg slightly further back behind the girth (about one hand span), for example when riding circles.

-Indicate a change in direction with the lateral driving leg on the girth, for turning on the forehand or leg yielding.

-Behind the girth for half pirouette (turn on the haunches) and travers.

The extent to which these 'influ-

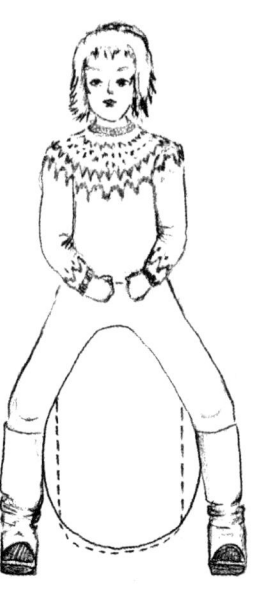

If the horse is tense (broken line), it feels like it is holding its breath. The muscles are tight, the horse's body doesn't 'fill' the rider whose legs can't make contact with the horse's flanks and therefore can't apply leg aids.

The relaxed (solid line) horse keeps a supple body, makes it easy for the rider to apply leg aids and is almost offering him a rhythm in which to do so.

ences' depend upon each other and interact to become 'aids' should become clear from the following example. If the influence of the rider's leg is detached from the global and harmonious concept of the aids, it is completely immaterial to the horse whether the impulse of the lateral or forward driving leg works directly on the girth or behind it. The position of the leg is crucial only in connection with seat aids, which we

Training the rider

If the horse is in a pacey tölt, then the rider has to brace himself against the movement. His legs slip forward and he can hardly keep them still. One can often see a rhythmical swinging of the ankles in an attempt to capture the movement. The pronounced lateral action of the horse's back is throwing the rider from side to side. We do not feel it is possible to use pelvic aids correctly in this situation.

What the rider feels

Until the horse can move in a supple way, it often looks to the attentive observer or the sensitive rider as if it is holding its breath. A tense horse is either stubborn, or slow to react, or will simply run away with the rider. The horse does not 'fill the rider', as this feeling is also described. His legs do not seem to be able to make contact with the flanks.

Icelandic Horse riders are familiar with another unpleasant feeling: the horse is in a pacey tölt and riders can hardly keep their legs from slipping forward, because the pronounced lateral movement of the horse's back does not allow them to sit properly.

The other extreme is the rider who grips tightly with his legs, thus automatically losing the influence of his seat. As a consequence of tense squeezing with the lower legs, the seat bones are lifted out of the saddle.

It is also pointless for tall riders on extremely small, barrel-shaped horses to pull their legs up, as this will stiffen the whole seat. Owners of such horses – and this is actually a recommendation to all riders – should buy a saddle with a narrow sitting area which does not force the upper thighs too far apart.

The Seat

Let us divide this into two parts to make things clearer.

will deal with later. Let's just say for now that only a correctly placed leg allows the rider to adopt the correct position for riding turns. This position we will call the 'swivel seat'. It is the leg that will ensure that the rider is not destroying the forward impulse created by the seat.

Weight

Two-thirds of the rider's weight 'rests' on the seat bones and the buttocks. The remaining third is distributed evenly on both sides of the horse, from the upper thighs to the stirrups. Compared with the range of possibilities for leg and hand aids, and the use of the back, the variety of influences using just weight is relatively small. The rider has little room for freedom of movement and can only shift his weight slightly forwards, backwards or laterally.

In order for both partners, four and two legged, to be able to work together in harmony, their respective centres of gravity must always be in unison, a connection that creates one single line of gravity. If the rider is not doing his part, the horse is forced to counterbalance his dead weight thus upsetting its own self-carriage and becoming stiff in the long run.

The swivel seat

A rider who wants to lay down the basis for harmonious riding must place the saddle precisely over the horse's centre of gravity. In addition to that, he needs to be able to apply the principles of the so-called 'swivel seat' to all other sitting positions. We differentiate between the basic seat, the relief seat (where the rider's seat bones remain in contact with the saddle, but he angles his upper body forward towards the horse's neck), and the forward seat (where the seat bones are not in contact with the saddle anymore, but the weight is carried by the upper thighs and the stirrups and the upper body is leaning forward towards the horse's neck).

The swivel seat, in simplified terms, requires the rider's shoulders to be parallel to the horse's shoulders and his hips parallel to the horse's hips; remaining that way in circles and turns. This will keep the rider's weight on the inside at all times. Turns in fast tempo, for example, will then not result in the centrifugal force throwing his weight to the outside, for which the horse would have to compensate, causing it unnecessary tension. The swivel seat prevents the hips from 'collaps-

Whether riding in straight lines or in bends, the rider can use seat aids only when the horse's centre of gravity and his own can be connected by one line.

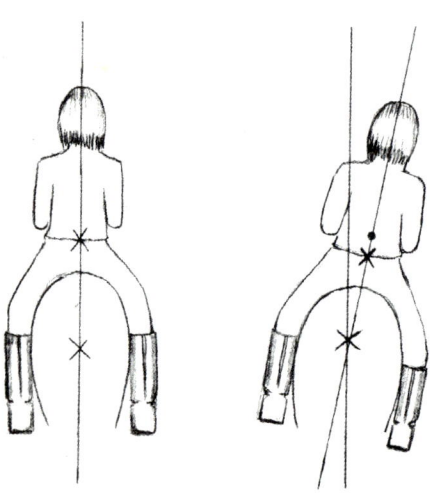

ing' and therefore allows even distribution of weight.

To achieve the swivel seat, in preparation for a turn, the rider's inner hip must be pushed forward and the inner shoulder taken slightly back in effect turning both shoulder and hip in opposite directions. This swivel movement automatically brings legs and hands into the most effective position for giving precise aids. The outer hip takes the leg back, taking some weight off the outer seat bone, while the outer shoulder takes the outer hand forward.

What the rider feels
Getting the feel for the correct swivel seat can be practised initially on a standing and then a walking horse. By seating himself alternately, so that first the right and then the left side becomes the inside, the rider will be more clearly aware of the weight difference between inner (heavy) and outer (light) seat bone. He will then experience a rhythmical feeling of the inner hip pushing forward and of his weight on the inner seat bone. Memorising this will help his further training.

The Back

In theory it should be possible for a rider to simply have his weight carried around by the horse and, by applying the swivel seat and a relaxed position, to barely interrupt the back-to-front flow of movement. On the other hand, the rider can support the flow of movement, make life easier for the horse and produce a nicer outline by using the influence of the lower back.

To do this we need an upright pelvis, lower legs lying softly against the horse's sides and a relaxed

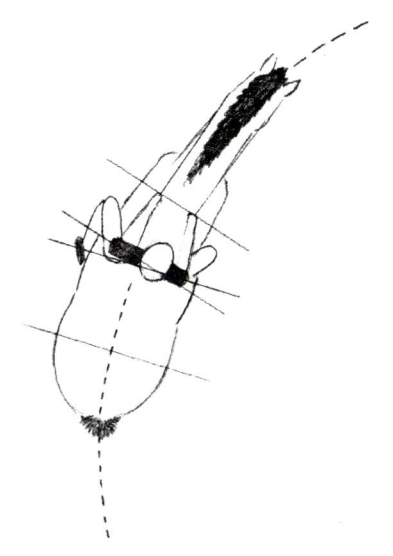

A swivel seat enables the rider to apply the correct seat aids (weight and pelvis) at all times. In simplified terms, it requires the rider's shoulders to be parallel to those of the horse and hips parallel to the horse's hips at all times. When riding a turn, the rider has to put more weight on the inner seat bone. He drives the horse with his inside leg on the girth and takes his outside leg about a hand span behind the girth to contain the movement (this automatically takes some weight off the outer seat bone). By almost leading the horse into the turn with the inner rein and balancing the bend with the outer, the rider is taking his inside shoulder back and his outer swivels forward.

Training the rider

The basics of pelvic aids are an upright pelvis, lower legs lying softly against the horse's sides and a relaxed shoulder position. The rider then deliberately increases the movement of his pelvis, which is swinging loosely with the rhythm of the horse, as if trying to press his seat bones firmly towards the front of the saddle.

shoulder position. The rider then deliberately increases the movement of his pelvis, which is swinging loosely with the rhythm of the horse, as if trying to press the seat bones firmly towards the front of the saddle. This is assisted by lengthening the legs.

Understanding the influence of the pelvis is rather difficult, since using the pelvis rarely results in a direct and obvious reaction. Nevertheless, the awareness of the activity in the lower back and the pelvic influence can be regarded as key factors in transmitting the flow of movement from the hindquarters through the back and neck to the front. These key factors will ensure harmonious and supple riding at all times. With an easy, relaxed, but upright position, every rider can significantly improve his chances of reaching this goal.

We feel it is almost impossible for a rider to use his lower back effectively on a stiff and predominantly

Training the rider   19

The rider can assess if his hips swing correctly for the pelvic aid by placing his hand on his waistband and concentrating on a regular rhythm. If he has hollowed his back, the movement swings only slightly forward from the vertical. With a rounded back, his hand will only feel a slight movement backward from the vertical.

laterally moving horse (see also the section on Back Aids). This lateral movement pushes the rider's leg forward and makes it difficult for him to swing his hip forward in tune with the rhythm. If the rider reacts by bracing himself against the stirrups, he automatically forces his seat backwards and out of the saddle.

Hunched shoulders intensify this negative effect. Tensely squared shoulders, on the other hand, lead to a hollow back, and again, the rider denies himself the chance of developing supple and forward swinging hips.

What the rider feels
Whenever a rider wants to check the swinging of his hips (the basis for the pelvic aid), he can, either in walk or trot, place the back of his hand against his lower back, just above the waistband. In the basic seat, he should feel his spine move evenly to and fro, in complete unison with the rhythm of the horse's movement. If the rider hollows his back, the detected movement swings only slightly forward from the vertical. In a rounded back, his hand will only feel a slight movement backward

from the vertical. In both cases, free swinging with the movement of the horse's back is not possible.

The Hands

The final link in the chain is the rider's hands. The movement which flows like a wave from the hindquarters and on through the whole body of the horse is ultimately taken up, transformed and sent back by the hands.

Because of their mobility and versatility, the hands are one of the most sensitive tools in the communication between rider and horse. It must be noted that the horse's mouth is very sensitive and extremely vulnerable. For this reason, many trainers try to completely avoid any negative rein influence by constantly reminding their pupils to keep their hands still. Yet the very command 'Keep your hands still!' leads to tension in the rider and the hands become rigid and hard. It is simply not possible for the hands to be the only part of the body to be kept still, when the rider is otherwise moving rhythmically with the horse. If he does not want to lose an important tool for directing the horse towards harmonious co-operation, the rider must incorporate the hands into the flow of movement.

The elastic hand

The rider must try to let his hands swing with the rhythm of the horse's

The rider's hands must also be in harmony with the movement. He allows his hands to follow the rhythm of the horse's gently nodding head and applies aids in the rhythm of the movement. Worst possible mistake: the rider tries to keep his hands still and his aids become rigid and tense.

gently nodding head, following the constant to and fro of the horse's nose, to achieve a soft and even contact with the reins.

Once he has memorised this nodding sensation and it has become almost second nature for the hands to swing automatically with the movement of the horse, he is then ready to incorporate the aids in the rhythm of the movement.

If the rider wants to 'give with the reins', his hands will emphasise a move forward towards the horse's mouth. If he wants to 'take with the reins' his hands will emphasise a backward movement towards his pelvis, which at the same time is pushing forward. If the rider applies a half halt at every swing, he will influence the hindlegs alternately. He can also – in a similar way to rising trot – use every other swing for a half halt, thus directing a specific influence towards one particular hindleg.

As the horse advances in its training, the forward and backward swing of the rider's hands will become less noticeable. Now the movement of horse and rider are so in tune, the contact so light and elastic, that it looks to the observer as if the hands are still. This effect develops as the movement of the horse's head decreases and its self carriage increases and, with the poll being the highest point of the neck, gives the illusion that the horse is 'stepping through the poll'.

In difficult exercises like piaffes, the rider will need to move his hands slightly up and down with the rhythm, in order to avoid tension. Note: rigid hands are far worse than hands that are not quite in tune. Basically, the rider should have the feeling that he is 'carrying' his hands

Typical faults with the rider's hands
If a horse avoids the bit by throwing its head up behind the vertical and pushing the underside of his neck out (almost giving the impression of a ewe neck), many riders try to force their horse back into a 'dressage type outline' by pulling the hands right down on either side of the withers. This cannot produce the desired effect, for the following reason: a horse with its head raised behind the vertical simultaneously hollows its back. Now the back and the neck muscles cannot co-operate any more to allow the movement to flow through to the neck and head. Our wave from back to front has been stopped. The rider who tries to correct this problem by forcing his hands downwards will, at the same time, give up his driving seat as the upper body tips forward and the seat becomes detached from the movement. The rider has now effectively deprived himself and the horse of the opportunity to transport more energy through the back into the hand, in order to correct this bad outline. But it doesn't stop there. A downward pull of the hands results

in painful pressure on the horse's jaw and will encourage the horse to apply counter-pressure. The lower muscles reaching from the abdomen, through the underside of the horse's neck, to the jaw, become more and more developed through exercise, and the 'ewe neck' becomes more pronounced.

The only way to combat this problem successfully is for the rider to follow the horse's mouth upwards with his hands. At the same time, the use of his legs, weight and back must encourage the horse to round its back, therefore 'repairing' the lost connection. Now enough energy can be transported from the quarters, through the back and neck to enable the horse to correct itself towards the ideal position of 'stepping through the poll'.

It is just as difficult to pull a horse's head up as it is to pull it down. Horses that 'creep' behind the

A rider who pushes his hands low denies the horse any chance to relax its head and neck into a lower outline. Because of this 'fight' the rider assists in strengthening the lower muscles in the horse's neck. When the horse finally gives in, it will also have dropped its shoulders and come onto the forehand, all because it wasn't given a chance to relax its back, due to being forcefully pulled down. The right approach would be: the rider takes up a supple seating position, raises his hands higher, tries to apply effective driving aids and waits patiently until the horse reaches for the bit and drops its nose.

vertical – seemingly biting themselves in the chest – are only trying to evade a rough hand. A rider trying to correct this position by lifting his hands merely intensifies this feared sensation, giving the horse even more reason to stay behind the bit. The right way to correct this is by riding the horse forward into a positive contact with a forward feeling in the reins, a relatively low hand lightly following the nodding movement of the head.

Possible influences of the hands
The rider can use his hands in a variety of ways.

He can 'give with the reins', that is let the hands follow the motion, keeping an elastic contact (when moving off). He can 'hold with the reins', that is remaining still against the movement of the horse (used, for instance, in the half halt). He can 'take with the reins', that is momentarily applying pressure with the reins, taking his hands backwards in the rhythm of the movement (used, for instance, when 'holding' didn't produce the desired result in the half halt). Or he can finally 'restrain', that is a one-sided 'taking with the reins' when the aim is to contain the movement in a bend or turn.

What the rider feels
Until an elastic and sympathetic hand has become second nature, the rider must make a point of concentrating on his movements. He should initially move his hands at least ten centimetres (4 inches) back and forth in every gait until he is able to find the rhythm. Care should be taken to only ever use a backward swing for a half halt. Finally, the rider can quite deliberately swing his hands in unison with the movement of each individual hindleg, or – similar to posting – only swing to every second beat. He should also frequently alternate his swing, just as he does in rising trot.

The Combined Use of the Aids

It is essential that the rider has understood the principle of how to create and control the flow of movement within the horse: from the legs, through the seat (weight and back) forward to the hands......... Only then will he be able to comprehend the harmonious interaction of the aids.

Translated into an example of a conversation, the correct combination of the aids will be received by the horse as a suggestion or a command. By using aids at the right time and in the correct dosage (rider's tact), the rider can successfully 'persuade' his horse to carry out the desired exercise.

Half halt

The rider should make a point of beginning every 'conversation' with his horse with a half halt. If this initial overture is neglected and the half halt doesn't happen, then the following exercise will probably put excessive demands on the horse from the outset. That makes the half halt roughly the equivalent to the speaker's discrete tapping on his wine glass when he wants to make a speech at the dinner table and needs to get the attention of his audience. It not only serves the purpose of answering the question: "is the horse ready to comply to the rider's slightest wish?" but also enables the rider to check his own position (his 'command centre'). Are his legs, his seat and hands correctly placed to be able to start a clear dialogue with the horse?

As a lesson, the half halt can be subdivided into two phases of motion that will be executed almost simultaneously. Both legs on the girth (perhaps even a little further back), weight on the seat bones pushing the hips forward, driving the horse momentarily against the 'holding' reins. In the second phase, the driving seat is given up for a passive swinging with the movement of the horse, whilst the reins briefly release before restoring original contact.

The rider can now lighten the rein contact, but only so far as the horse will follow the bit in a forward/downward movement. If the horse grabs the bit and pulls down, or becomes tense and tries to avoid rein contact by raising its head (in other words, although the rider gives with the reins, the horse does not follow forward/downward, but keeps its head up), then the rider has to start with the half halt all over again.

The effect of the half halt
The half halt enables the rider to control his influence on the

The half halt can be divided into two phases of motion executed almost simultaneously. In the first phase, the rider drives the horse with seat and legs against 'guarding' reins to achieve collection. In the second phase, the rider lets the horse stretch a little to enable its back muscles to relax, despite engaged hindquarters. This 'giving' is followed again by phase one. The rider has to apply half halts in quick succession in order to achieve his goal, especially at the start of the training

1.

hindquarters and thus the suppleness of the horse. He can use this exercise to improve attentiveness, rhythm, self carriage and balance, as well as riding downward transitions, for example to change from canter to trot or from a fast to a slow tölt.

The half halt can only be considered successful if the horse, in the second phase, is willingly stretching forward with the giving reins and thus expands its outline and relaxes its back. Unfortunately, Icelandic Horse shows still have their 'Natural Tölt Test 1.1' which incorporates a 'tölt on a loose rein' section. For some strange reason, judges want to see the horse carry on tölting with a high head carriage, unsupported by the reins. A horse that has learned to follow the hands and the bit and to relax and stretch whenever this aid is applied (which of course is important later for riding flying pace) will simply be confused by this demand.

Faults in riding the half halt
If the rider executes the second phase carelessly or completely 'forgets' to release the holding rein, then a supple and well-trained horse will stop or even move backwards. Another may become tense and push against the standing hand.

By releasing the reins, the rider is giving the horse the opportunity to relax its back, a reward after the previous impulse that created a better self carriage and collection.

Measured application of the aids and also use of the half halt does not only have to be learned by the rider. For the horse, it can also be a fairly long process until it has accomplished a relaxed half halt, re-balancing itself, even at the highest level of collection. It is extremely important for the rider not to regard the half halt as a trick or an obedience exercise which is practised time and again, until the horse has

2.   3.   4.

26 Training the rider

The rider is applying the emergency brake, instead of applying a half halt. He is bracing himself against the stirrups, is gripping with his upper thighs and is giving up his pelvic influence. The horse's flow of movement is rudely interrupted. The hindlegs leap frantically and completely uncoordinated beneath the centre of gravity, the back is rigid. It will be impossible for the horse to shorten its outline smoothly.

finally caught on. The half halt, like the full halt, is always the result of successful suppling-up exercises in the warming up phase.

Full halt

The full halt – which is made up of several half halts and leads from every gait or tempo to a complete stop – tells us just about everything about the suppleness of a horse.

Does the horse slow down smoothly and come to a halt without a 'stop' or a 'jerk'? Is the movement right up to the halt fluent and light? Do the quarters carry more and more weight by evenly stepping under the body? If so, the rider has achieved his goal: he has trained his 'dream horse'.

Faults in the full halt

There is one thing the trainer should always be aware of: if the horse does not accept the half halt, then it will fail in the full halt as well. If it seems to become stubborn against the hand, this is not usually because of a lack of obedience, but because the horse is still tense and the aids can't flow through. Riding transitions, changing gaits and tempi and other loosening exercises will help both partners much more than violently hitting the 'emergency brake', which unfortunately is seen far too often. For a rider to 'pull' with all his strength against a horse, he must grip tightly with his upper thighs and knees, or even stand in the stirrups. As a result, his seat bones lift out of the saddle and he loses the influence of his back. This interrupts the flow even more and the horse has little chance to relax his back.

Quite often one sees demonstrations of sudden 'stops' executed by apparently supple and obedient horses. Skilled riders are forcing their horses to a stop within a few metres, often from high speed. A closer look reveals how the hindlegs leap frantically under the centre of gravity in a completely uncoordinated and choppy movement – a certain sign of a horse that is not supple in the back and therefore unable to shorten its outline smoothly.

Another mistake, often seen when observing novice riders, is that the full halt leaves the horse on the forehand. Not enough forward impulsion was created, the horse cannot take up the weight with its quarters, becomes low in the shoulders, and stops on the forehand, often visibly pulling down on the bit.

Rein back

One could call reining back 'the highest level' of the full halt. After having been brought to attention by a half halt, the horse moves backwards, raising and setting down its legs in almost simultaneous diagonal pairs whilst maintaining a regular rhythm. The rider applies the aids to move forward, but the reins restrain the forward movement. The aids are similar to the half halt or halt – with both legs slightly behind the girth, weight on the seat bones, pushing the hips forward and driving the horse against the 'holding' reins.

The signs of a correctly executed rein back and a supple horse can be easily recognised when the horse is not tipping backwards, and is raising its legs as if about to step forward, but then places them backwards.

The rein back requires a horse with well-developed back muscles and quarters that are able to carry the body mass smoothly. The rider can initially make it easier for the horse by tipping his upper body slightly forward, putting more weight on the thighs and into the stirrups, thus easing the weight in the saddle. This will permit the horse to arch its back upwards, which will in turn make it easier to step back.

Moving backwards is a collection exercise because it engages the hindquarters. It enables the rider to check if his combined aids are getting through and is ultimately an obedience exercise.

Faults in the rein back
It is precisely this last point which leads many riders to use the rein back as a punishment. Crudely applied, the horse will react frantically; it will rush or even attempt to jump back and has no chance of relaxing its back. This is very similar to the 'stops' mentioned in the full halt.

The other extreme is the horse that is given too little encouragement initially to go forward. There is no impulsion and the horse creeps backwards, dragging its legs and keeping its shoulders low, thus making it impossible to engage its hindquarters.

Basic Exercises

Besides the elementary half halts, there are other exercises available to the rider, where using the correct combination of aids can improve a harmonious relationship with the horse.

Moving off

After a half halt has prepared the horse for the fact that the rider now expects something from it, the rider asks for forward movement by applying pressure with both legs on the girth, keeping his weight on the seat bones. The reins maintain a light contact. If the rider wants to move off in a faster gait and for any other upward transition, then the opening half halt must be more pronounced to ensure the full attention of the horse.

Faults when moving off
Frequently, the half halt is forgotten prior to moving off, or done so carelessly that it doesn't have the required effect. The horse's first step takes it straight into a negative movement (see also chapter on self-carriage), as it almost stumbles forward. The horse is now either tensing up or becoming unbalanced and in any subsequent exercise, the rider is hindered by his own initial negligence.

Even if, before moving off, the half halt lacks just a little fine tuning in the delicate giving and taking of the reins, the rider may well have difficulty in executing exercises with a horse that is either tense or that lacks impulsion.

Changes of direction – Riding turns

After the introduction with a half halt, the horse is positioned in the direction of the turn. The rider assumes a swivel seat: inside leg drives on the girth, outside leg is slightly further back (one hand span), containing the movement and determining the degree of the bend. The seat bones are turned in order to stay central in the saddle, thus putting more weight on the inner seat bone and pushing the inner hip and pelvis forward into the movement. The inside rein asks for a slight bend, whereas the outside rein limits the bend of the neck and head.

Faults in riding turns

The most obvious mistake when riding turns is that the horse is evading the aids for a supple bend of the whole body, by falling out at the shoulders. On the stiff side, the inner shoulder and on the soft side, the outer shoulder will be affected. (For correction see the section on natural crookedness).

A fault one sees very often is the rider who tries to position his horse for bending inwards but does not take his inside hand into the bend. In the most extreme cases he will even pull his hand over the horse's neck towards the outside, trying to prevent the horse from coming in too far. However, this movement automatically brings the rider's inner shoulder forward, weight on the inner seat bone is lost, and the swivel seat becomes ineffective. The rider is sitting correctly when, by turning his shoulders to the inside, his movement is taking his upper body with the inner hand slightly back, allowing the inner rein to establish the bend. His outer shoulder comes forward and with it the outside hand, allowing the outside rein to follow the movement of the horse's head and neck into the bend.

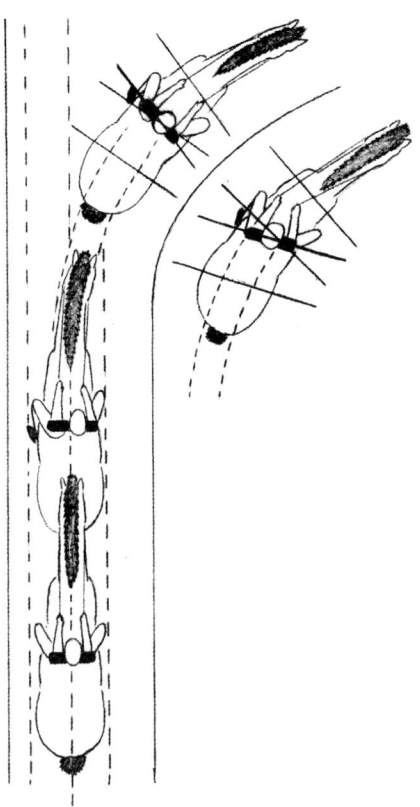

The rider on the left is applying the swivel seat, for instance in a corner. He is keeping his shoulders parallel to the horse's shoulder and his hips parallel to the horse's hips. This places his weight in the best position to apply aids and gives the horse the opportunity to relax.

The rider on the right is exhibiting one of the most common mistakes when riding bends. In order to soften the horse on the inside, he will pull his inside hand over the horse's neck, towards the outside. The result: he abandons the swivel seat (his shoulder is no longer parallel to the horse's shoulder) and the effectiveness of his aids is lost. His weight hangs to the outside and the horse cannot relax.

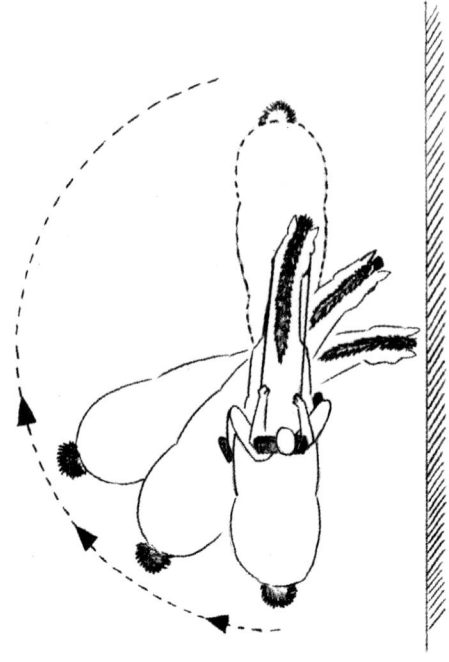

In the turn on the forehand, the horse is learning to react to the leg aid by moving sideways. Because the hindquarters are moving away from the combined centre of gravity, it is better to drop this exercise as soon as the horse has understood this lateral movement.

movement. Increased weight is put on the inner seat bone, the pelvis is slightly tipped back as the rider pushes his inner hip into the forward movement. The inner rein positions the horse, the outside rein restrains the forward impulsion and helps to maintain balance.

Faults when riding the turn on the forehand

When attempting to turn on the forehand, it is often the case that the horse has been bent too far to the inside and in order to correct this, is simply pulled round with the inside rein. The rider must remember to let his inside leg be the dominant part of the aid, rather than the inside rein.

It should eventually be possible to make the horse understand the meaning of lateral leg pressure, either by working with the horse from the ground or with the assistance of a helper. The rider should also check his aids: the leg aid must always come first, before the rein aid.

The turn on the forehand

The horse's hindquarters rotate, in the rhythm of the walk, around the forehand. The turn on the forehand gives both horse and rider a chance to develop a feeling for lateral aids. After a half halt the rider asks for a slight bend to the inside, applies pressure with his inside leg on the girth. The outside leg is slightly behind the girth and contains the

Leg yielding

Leg yielding is an exercise that will help horse and rider to develop a feel for the lateral leg aids. This exercise is only beneficial for a certain period, that is, until the horse has learned to react to lateral leg pressure, and the swivel seat has become second nature to the rider. If the horse accepts the outside leg correctly (that maintains forward

Training the rider

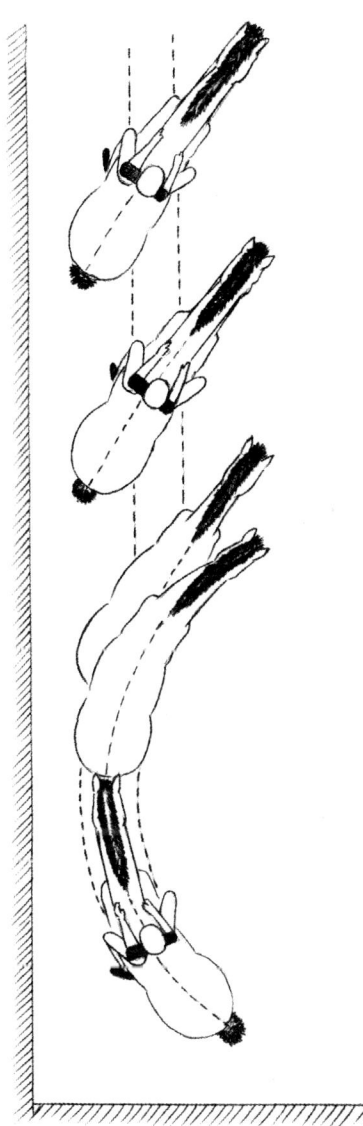

movement and keeps the horse straight) and the outside rein (that regulates the bend and stops the shoulder from falling out), then the exercise can be dropped from the training programme. Leg yielding has no gymnastic benefit in itself, because the hindquarters, moving away from the combined centre of gravity (of horse and rider), are not encouraged to carry more weight.

Aids for leg yielding
The rider adopts a swivel seat, turning as he positions the horse. Because of the weight distribution,

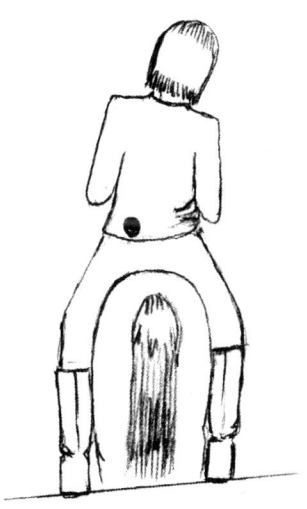

Leg yielding is also an exercise that teaches the rider the use of a laterally driving leg and teaches the horse to react correctly. This exercise is only beneficial until a swivel seat and its effect has become second nature.

The most frequently seen posture problem when riding bends or leg yielding is a collapsed hip. The result: the rider's centre of gravity (●) slips towards the outside and his weight distribution is wrong. The horse has no chance to react to a laterally driving leg in a relaxed manner, because it has to counter balance the rider's weight.

the inner leg now applies pressure on the girth, or is, at least, placed further forward than the outside leg, asking the horse for an inside bend. The weight is on the inner seat bone, and therefore on the inside, the rider's inner hip is pushed forward with increased pelvic movement on the inside. He bends the horse to the inside with the inner rein, while the outer rein regulates and prevents the shoulder from falling out.

Faults in leg yielding

In leg yielding especially, we can often see how the rider fails to apply a correct swivel seat. The result is that the rider's weight is thrown to the wrong side and he deprives the horse of the chance to react correctly to a laterally driving leg.

Another problem we see quite often is the failure of the initial half halt at the beginning of the exercise. The horse is not collected, is too long in the frame and the outside shoulder is falling out. Especially on the hollow, supposedly soft side, horses simply 'race' forward, overbending their necks hugely. This is a sure sign that the outside aids are completely missing.

Incorrect leg yielding from the stiff side almost always results in the hindquarters leading. The natural flow of movement from back to front is therefore interrupted and the horse can't relax. In this case, the rider should ease the rein aids and concentrate more on riding forward.

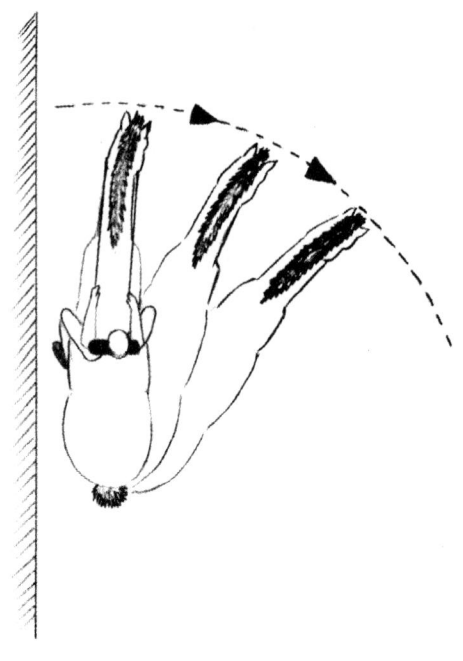

The turn on the haunches is an exercise in collection because the horse has to bring its quarters increasingly under the combined centre of gravity. The horse is positioned into the bend. The rider sits in the correct swivel seat and therefore has, in this exercise, his weight on the inside.

Turn on the haunches (half pirouette)

The horse's forehand moves around the haunches in the rhythm of walk. The half pirouette is an exercise in collection, giving the rider the opportunity to encourage the horse's hindquarters to accept more weight. The quarters have to move from the outside towards the inside in order to stay underneath the centre of gravity, as the weight of horse and rider shifts towards the inside during the exercise.

Preparation for the turn on the haunches is, as usual, a half halt. The horse is then positioned into the bend, so that it looks in the direction in which it is going. The direction in which the horse goes is subsequently the inside. The rider adopts a swivel seat: inside leg on the girth – that maintains the forward movement and bends the horse. Outside leg is about a hand span behind the girth, – driving laterally. Increased weight on the inner seat bone, inner hip pushed forward – which will automatically engage the inside of the pelvis. The inner rein obtains and maintains the bend of the horse. The outer rein, by applying half halts, takes the forehand around the hindquarters.

Faults in riding the turn on the haunches

Unfortunately, the turn on the haunches very often looks as follows: for the first two or three steps, the forehand moves around the haunches which remain motionless, instead of rhythmically moving on the spot. Thereafter, the horse abandons the inside bend and continues in counter position, similar to the movement seen in leg yielding. The haunches are moving now, but in the wrong direction. The horse has to be ridden in this counter position during the second part of the exercise, in order to produce any lateral movement at all. In this example, the rider's outside aids haven't been effective, the active forward impulsion has been neglected and his half halt, at the beginning of the exercise, wasn't carried through. (For correction, see the section on training the horse)

Training the Horse

"Time" is the main factor when it comes to training. Once rider and horse are on the right track, it is only a question of time until the horse turns into a Gæðingur, a dream horse. The training of a horse that is not blessed with natural talent can take a very long time. A talented horse on the other hand, can make it very easy for the rider. In this chapter, we have deliberately not mentioned any time scale in connection with training. The time that has to be invested in the different stages is not only different from horse to horse, but also the experience and sensitivity of the trainer plays an important role.

However, once on the right track, tasks which formerly seemed impossible can be mastered and the patient rider will reach his goal. He has to ask himself two questions before beginning his work. Do I really want to invest this amount of time? Have I found the right horse that, for my purposes, has the appropriate talent?

Time is the main factor when it comes to training a young horse. Rhythm and suppleness is the first goal for the trainer before he can concentrate on getting the horse collected.

To start with, the rider must devote enough time to handling his horse so that they form a proper bond with each other. Professional riders often overlook how important a good emotional relationship is. Often they might not be able to dedicate the necessary time, either for financial or other reasons, but they work at such a high level that they can get a lot out of a horse simply because of their superior ability.

The rider's priority in training the horse should be its welfare. It all starts with providing decent shelter

and adequate paddock space. In addition to this, work should be imaginative and tailored to the surroundings. This means that those who don't have access to a riding arena have to think of an alternative. The same is true for people who have no hacking country to speak of or no access to an oval track. Using the old proverb: "the soil moulds its people", one could argue that the riding country shapes the horse, or at least its training. For example, a trainer in Iceland who has vast spaces at his command will initially not bother too much about his horse's obedience. His riding country allows him to ride flat out for long distances without any risks. In more densely populated countries, it could prove life threatening to postpone basic obedience training.

The Introductory Stage – Laying the Foundations

Every horse has to undergo the same basic training, no matter whether it is destined for a career in competition, leisure riding, or whether it is going to earn its keep as a riding school horse. This work should only be undertaken by an experienced rider, (if possible with the guidance of an instructor), as mistakes that are made in the basic training are very difficult to correct later.

Depending on where and how the horse grew up, the initial step will be either to teach the shy horse that it's all right to be caught or to teach the bold one to be respectful of people. The most important principle in training is: as soon as the horse has made the slightest attempt to obey a command, it has to be praised immediately. 'Praise' doesn't mean that you have to fling your arms around its neck every time. An immediate 'Good boy or girl', 'Yes' or a similar word is enough, and it can work wonders!

Grooming, picking out the feet, or leading to the 'work place' are the first shared exercises for horse and rider and the latter can almost be regarded as the first step of groundwork.

Groundwork

Leading

Leading a horse in walk or trot, straight or around bends, in turns on the forehand and moving backwards, are all groundwork exercises where the horse is expected to react to minute signals from the handler. For groundwork, the horse should be fitted with a head collar. The trainer should use a chain with a lead attached. It is crucial that the chain is fitted correctly: threaded from the outside through the lower near side ring of the head collar, crossing the noseband once, it should come out from the inside of

Training the horse

The serious side of life starts here. Leading is the first lesson during groundwork. The trainer walks beside the horse's shoulder and guides it with voice, chain and a longish schooling whip.

the lower ring on the off side. Now the chain is taken up to the upper ring, still on the off side, and fastened there. The chain should only be used with a little tug or a vibrating movement to get attention, or to collect the horse. It should never be used forcefully or as punishment. The trainer now walks beside the horse's shoulder and guides it with his voice, the chain and a schooling whip of about 120 cm in length. In the early stages it might be advantageous for the trainer to have an assistant, also equipped with a longish whip, who helps to control forward movement. The whip is thought of as an extension of the trainer's arm, to be used as a signal and for guidance only.

This work from the ground should be repeated until the horse has learned to accept the driving whip and the collecting chain, and appears to understand the voice commands of the trainer.

After these groundwork exercises, the horse should be brought back into the stable where a well fitting bridle should be put on (no noseband straps fastened) before the horse is fed. In this way, it has a chance to become familiar with the bit and not learn to put its tongue

Training the horse

Starting groundwork - the horse is wearing a head collar. The trainer influences the horse with the help of a chain. The chain is threaded from the outside through the lower nearside ring of the head collar, crossing the noseband once (to make its effect softer), it comes out from the inside of the lower ring on the offside. Now the chain is taken up to the upper ring, still on the off side, and fastened there.

over it, as it is impossible for a horse to eat with its tongue over the bit. After about an hour, the bridle can be removed. When the horse has learned to eat with the bit, we can then proceed to the next stage of adding the saddle, again before feeding, and leaving the horse for a while.

Lungeing

Once horse and rider are in harmonious agreement when leading, then lungeing can be introduced. It is essential to have a well fenced lungeing circle of about 15 metres in diameter. If we are not attempting to correct a problem horse, it is probably enough just to put up a tape of some sort, about one metre high. The trainer initially uses the principle employed in leading, that is, pushing his horse from behind and walking with it in a smaller inner circle. In doing this, he encourages the horse to go forward and prevents the horse from pulling towards the outside and falling out over the shoulder in the process. This is exactly what would happen if he just stood in the middle and expected the horse to walk around him.

The work on the lunge begins in a faster gait – trot, tölt, pace or canter – depending on what the horse is offering. In this faster gait the trainer asks for a good tempo to make it easier for the novice horse to move forward freely. If the horse doesn't relax after a few rounds, is not drop- ping its neck and can't find a rhythm, the trainer should initially reduce the speed within the gait he is working in and only gradually increase the tempo. Depending on the type of horse, the first lungeing session could last as little as a few minutes. If the trainer feels that the horse loses his will to go forward, it is time to stop the exercise. The workload should only be increased

Applying the groundwork principle and driving the horse from behind, the trainer is lungeing his horse by walking in a smaller inner circle. Aids for slowing down are actually applied by moving in this inner circle ahead of the horse, and by positioning the lunge whip in front of the horse's head.

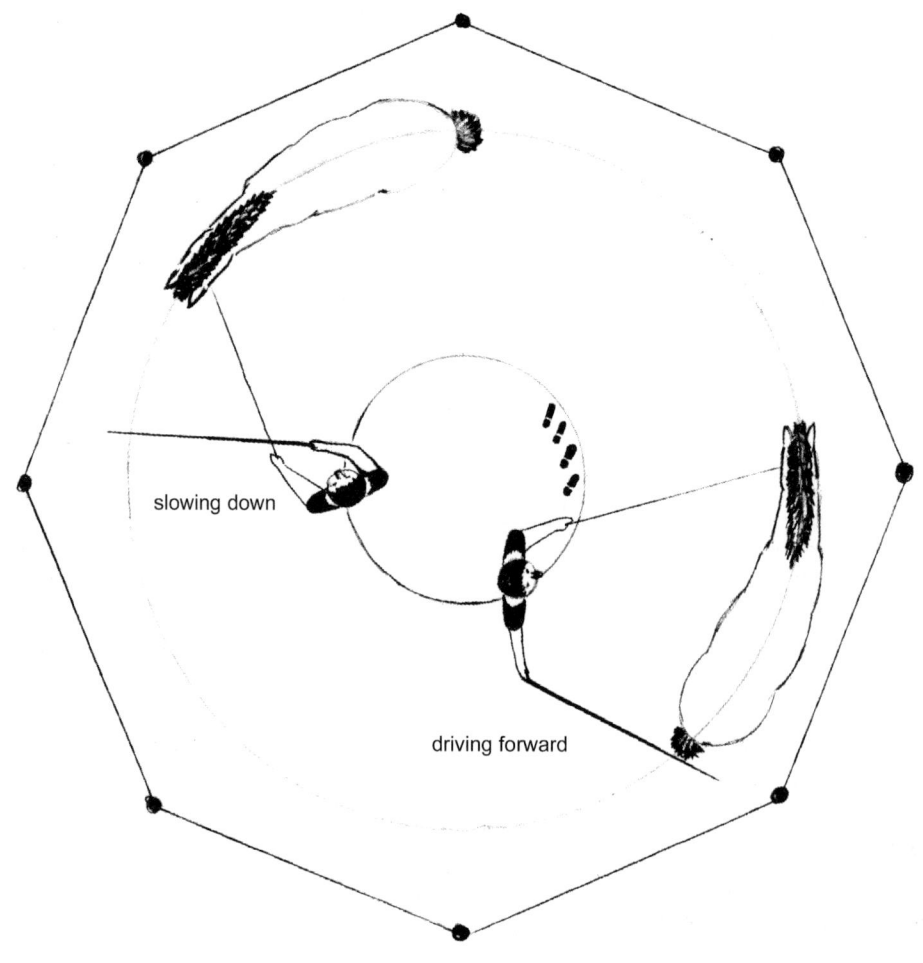

Training the horse

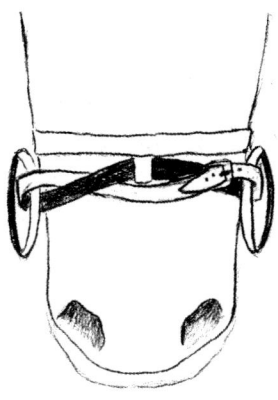

When lungeing in a bridle we use a flash noseband. The straps are not fastened under the chin, but are taken through both rings of the bit and done up on top of the horse's nose. Used in this way, it can prevent the horse putting its tongue over the bit and it also transfers the pressure of side reins or reins onto the top of its nose.

slowly and gradually. When the horse has learned to move freely forward on one rein, then it is time for the trainer to start working on the other rein.

To make the daily work programme easier for the horse, it should now be shod. It has been proved beneficial at the beginning of lunge training to initially only put shoes on the front feet and shoe the hind feet about 2 weeks later. This usually makes it easier for the horse to find its balance.

In these early workouts, the horse will only wear a head collar, perhaps with the chain attached. After a few days, the bridle can be put on top of the head collar, but the lunge rein should still be fastened to the halter. A little later the saddle is introduced, at first without stirrup irons or leathers. Depending on the shape of the horse, a front girth can be used to prevent the saddle from slipping forwards and eventually ending up under its belly, should the horse decide to buck.

Gait and tempi changes can now be gradually introduced into lunge work until the horse has learned to react to increasingly discreet signals of voice and whip.

Keeping the horse interested: leading the novice horse from another horse

To make work a bit more varied, the horse can now be taken out on hacks with a lead horse, still only wearing a head collar and chain attached to a lead rope. This should only be undertaken by an experienced rider, mounted on a placid and well-trained horse that is used to leading others. The assistance of a helper, who rides behind the novice horse to keep him going, is probably a good idea at first.

The next stage in lunge training is to do away with the head collar and work from the bridle. The use of a flash noseband with the lower flash strap not fastened as usual under the chin is recommended at first, but taken through the rings of a well fitting bit and fastened on top of the horse's nose. This not only lifts the bit in the horse's mouth, making it more difficult for the tongue to go over, but also transfers some of the pressure of any side rein onto the top of the nose. The lunge rein is clipped onto the bit ring. When lungeing the novice horse, use should be made of the outside boundary of the arena as guidance for the horse.

In these early stages the trainer has to ensure that the horse keeps its tongue under the bit. If there are any problems, then either the cheek pieces have to be shortened so they hold the bit higher up in the mouth, or the flash strap has to be tightened. If this fails, consider using a different bit altogether.

As soon as the horse has accepted the bit and is getting used to the general routine, the trainer can concentrate on the finer points, such as getting the horse supple, stretching forward/downwards and rounding its back. For this purpose, other training aids are used. Side reins, a balancing rein (sometimes called Equilonge) or draw reins have proved to be the most effective.

Purpose of lungeing
When working on the lunge, horse and rider will certainly become better acquainted. The horse will learn to react more smoothly to the signals of voice and whip. But the main objective for the horse is 'to find the way down', and to develop the strong back muscles it will need for its future job as a riding horse. Rather like the structure of a bridge

On the lunge, the horse has to learn to stretch forward and downward and reach for the bit. The trainer guides it with the use of draw reins (top), side reins (centre) or the Equilonge (bottom).

or an archway, the horse will be able to carry a rider in the most relaxed and efficient way if the head is lowered and the back is rounded. This position will also allow the hind legs to come underneath the body, engaging the quarters and, later, to take the combined weight of horse and rider. A considerate trainer will make sure that, before the horse is backed for the first time, its weight carrying ability has been built up in this way. An untrained, tense horse will lift its head and neck up high, which automatically hollows its back. The back muscles are now in a poor position to cope with the weight of the rider, leaving the horse in pain.

Gaits on the lunge
Whether on the lunge, schooling loose, or leading from another horse, the aim of the trainer is to get his horse working predominantly in trot as soon as possible. During groundwork, the walk should only be used to practise half halts, and in the early phase, canter work should be restricted to short periods. If the horse has difficulty cantering in a small circle, or gets tense and forever breaks into pace or disunited canter, it is probably best to cross the canter off the training programme for a while. After initially concentrating on perfecting the horse's training in trot, canter can then be added at a later date.

The five-gaiter can present a different problem on the lunge, by naturally offering tölt and pace. Here the trainer will try to persuade the

The purpose of lungeing is for the horse to lower its head and neck and to develop convex, weight bearing back muscles.

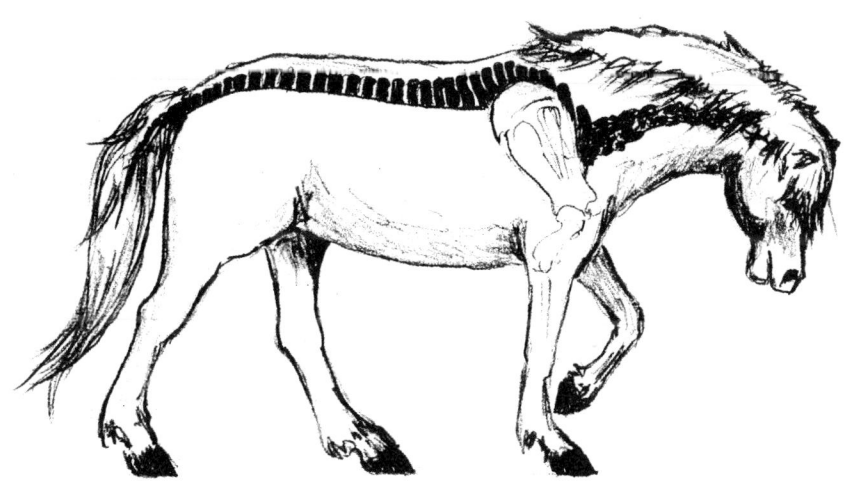

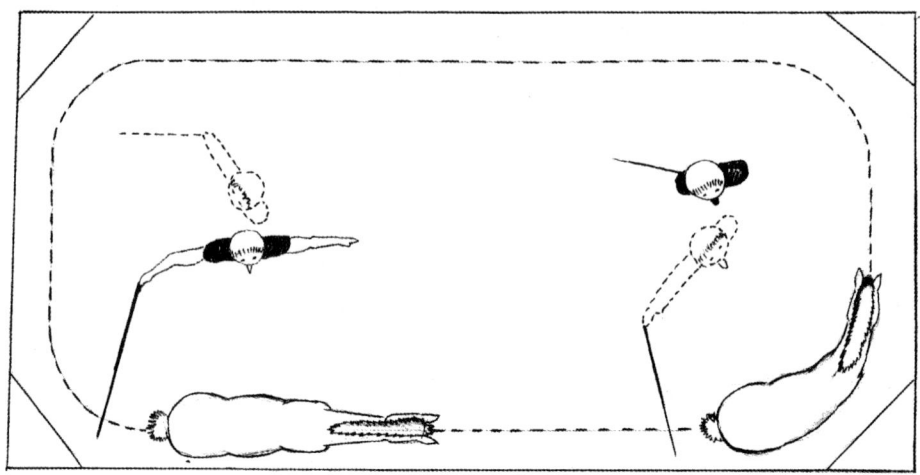

horse to trot by asking for constant changes in tempo. It is also quite common to see a five-gaiter in a slow four-beat canter. If the trainer succeeds in slowing this movement right down – a delicate and skilful affair – the horse might just slip into trot by itself. At the other end of the scale, we may find horses that trot only after the use of a balancing rein (Equilonge) or draw reins has taught them to lower their heads and necks.

Keeping the horse interested: loose schooling
To keep the work as varied as possible, the trainer might now consider schooling the horse loose in an indoor school, or in a safely fenced riding arena. If assisted by at least one helper, it is quite possible to practise the same exercises and signals as in lungeing, or even replace lungeing completely. The same

When loose schooling, the trainer should be assisted by at least one helper. Again, both 'trainers' are moving with the horse in a smaller inner circle (like in lungeing) and drive the horse from behind.

order as in lungeing should be followed. Start the horse initially with a head collar, then head collar and bridle, then head collar, bridle and saddle. Loose schooling is particularly recommended for trying to teach the five-gaiter to canter. The sheer size of an arena gives horses more room to move and generally allows them to find their balance – and sometimes the trot as well – much quicker.

Finally, being led from another horse might help the novice horse to learn the trot, as uneven ground conditions and changing scenery tend to influence horses towards the diagonal two-beat movement.

Starting the Young Horse

Backing

On the day of backing, the first objective should be to get the horse settled, best done by either working on the lunge, loose schooling or taking the novice out for a ride with a lead horse. The trainer might consider making the horse a little tired if he is expecting trouble when first mounting.

With the preparation work done and the horse tacked up, the trainer should then pull down the stirrup leathers, deliberately letting them swing against the horse's flanks, or even banging them against the boards of the riding arena. This should teach the horse that, despite all the commotion, nothing awful is going to happen. (But do make sure that a stirrup is not caught in the fencing!)

For the actual backing, the trainer will employ the services of an experienced rider who is able to stay with any movements the young horse may make. The horse should be positioned on the outer track of the arena or backed into a corner, but it is important to ensure that the horse can move off in a straight line. The trainer will now stand at a 45-degree angle in front of the horse's head. The rider, on the near side, adjusts the stirrups, approximately two or three holes shorter than usual, and gently secures the girth. The first step is to get the young horse used to the rider's weight. Carefully, with his foot in the stirrup, the rider will lean across the saddle and then slide quietly to the ground again, remaining beside the horse. This is repeated two or three times and the horse is praised and rewarded by the trainer on every occasion. When the horse

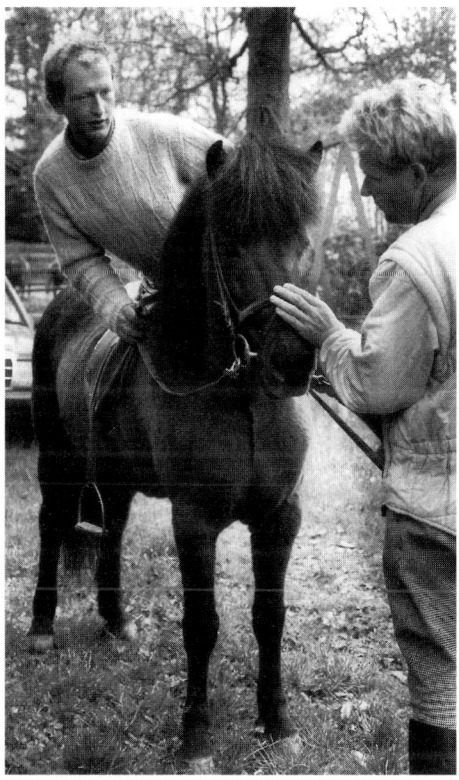

First mounting: the rider gets the horse used to his weight by putting his foot in the stirrup and carefully leaning across the saddle, then sliding quietly to the ground again. The trainer stands at the horse's head to stop any forward movement and talks to it reassuringly.

accepts this, the rider will proceed to swing his leg over the hindquarters and carefully glide into the saddle.

When the rider is sitting upright, with both feet in the stirrups, the trainer will walk the horse around the arena a couple of times. If all goes well, a lunge rein can be attached and the trainer proceeds with a 'normal' lungeing lesson. The rider takes up a relief seat, quietly following the horse's movements even if the horse initially speeds up a little. Most young horses realise pretty quickly that nothing is going to happen to them and will settle into a steady rhythm, even with the unfamiliar weight of the rider on their backs. It should be remembered that the rider is better off not talking to the horse during these first exercises. Sensitive animals might spook when they suddenly hear a voice from an unexpected direction.

In the next stage, the rider now takes the initiative more and more, gathering the reins. The trainer, still in charge of the lunge rein, will slowly recede into the background. Soon, the training can move from the lungeing circle to the riding arena – familiar surroundings the horse already knows from groundwork and loose schooling exercises.

The use of leg aids

By now the horse has learned, from the groundwork and lungeing sessions, to move forward when encouraged by the voice and the schooling whip. It is best to introduce the horse to leg aids when moving off. The rider asks for forward movement by initially applying even pressure with his legs on the girth, and immediately follows this with the familiar voice and whip commands. The horse will recognise this combination of aids quickly, soon anticipating that the leg aid is always followed by voice and whip signals and, with time, it will move forward straight after the leg is applied and will not wait for the 'second part'. Praising at exactly the right moment, when the horse reacts to the leg, is essential.

Riding out

If the horse is used to being outdoors, for instance if it has been taken out as a hand-horse, one can start to ride out on familiar tracks relatively soon. It is probably a good idea to take the horse on the lunge or give it a run in the school before venturing out. If the rider has had no opportunity to familiarise the horse with the surroundings, for example by taking it out with a lead horse, then he should walk the route of the intended first hack, leading the horse and perhaps integrating some groundwork exercises. In any case for the first few hacks, it is always advisable to be accompanied by another sensible rider on a reliable horse.

Initially, one should select a track where it is safe to let the horse go forward for a while, ideally in a relaxed trot or canter. The forward movement should not be restricted until the horse eases off slightly and the rider's aid is needed to keep the tempo. To reach this stage, it normally takes about ten to fifteen minutes. As soon as the rider feels he needs to drive the horse on, he can check his horse and return home at a walk.

Riders with nervous horses, which initially start work by running away in panic, have to develop an important skill – judging the physical fitness of their horse. One is easily tempted to put excessive demands on these horses, as they seem to offer a lot more than they are physically able to give, as a result of their fear. To be on the safe side, the horse's legs should be checked every day for signs of brushing or overreach injuries, splints or sprained tendons.

It is generally best if the rider places hacking-out on top of the agenda of his varied training programme. It's more fun for the horse than working in the school and it gives the rider the opportunity to influence the gaits (horses, for instance, prefer to trot in soft, deep ground) and improve balance.

The goal at this stage of training is to get the horse to go forward quietly but joyfully, with an ever-improving sense of balance. By now the use of side reins or a balancing rein (Equilonge) has served its purpose and the bridle can be used on its own.

This is not the time to try to correct problems of temperament with force. If the horse is pulling or showing too much will, then it is not a good idea to use the reins as a constant brake. It makes more sense to keep working the horse in the school, until the rider is put in the position where he can drive the horse forward. On the other hand, quieter horses with less will should be ridden out more and not worked in the school too often.

Very gradually, bending can now be integrated into the schooling work. The rider aims to perfect his half halts, practises striking off in canter in the corners, rides tempo transitions in all gaits and rehearses turns on the forehand and leg yielding.

The horse learns the halt

The rider will build on the fact that the horse is already familiar with calming voice commands from the groundwork exercises. He will initially still slow the horse by using his voice, but the reins will assist more and more in establishing the halt. The sooner the horse interprets the rein signals as a request to slow down, the easier it is for the rider to gradually introduce the correct combination of aids with legs, seat and reins.

The horse learns to turn

The rider is initially 'leading' his horse into the turn with the inner rein, moving his hand clearly towards the inside of the arena. His outside hand is holding a schooling whip, pointing forward to encourage the horse to turn, similar to the whip signals the horse is already familiar with from groundwork exercises. Very slowly, the signal with the schooling whip and 'leading' with the inner rein can be replaced by the correct aids.

The horse learns the turn on the forehand

The horse is taught the basic principles of the turn on the forehand during groundwork training. The changeover in lungeing is also done in a very similar way. The trainer stands beside the horse and gives a little tap with the schooling whip on the near quarters.

At the same time, a slight tug on the chain prevents the horse from moving forward and the horse steps to the side. This is the way to guide the quarters, step by step, around the forelegs. This exercise can also be done during a riding session, on the outside track of the school. The rider dismounts, positions himself on the track between the boards and the horse and guides the horse's hindlegs around the forelegs. Once the horse has understood what the

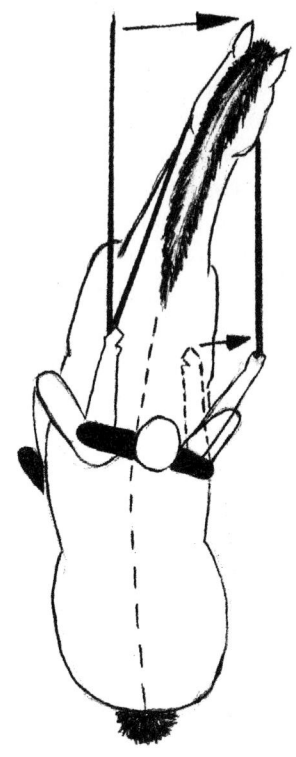

The horse learns to turn when the rider takes his inner hand clearly towards the inside of the turn (and therefore employs the correct swivel seat). His outside hand, combined with forward pointing schooling whip, contains the movement.

rider wants, the whole movement can be tried mounted, in a similar fashion to when the forward driving aids were introduced in moving off. The horse is halted squarely, about 1.5m off the track, to allow room for the head in the turn and then immediately turned. The boundary of the school initially helps the horse in the turn, naturally restricting its forward

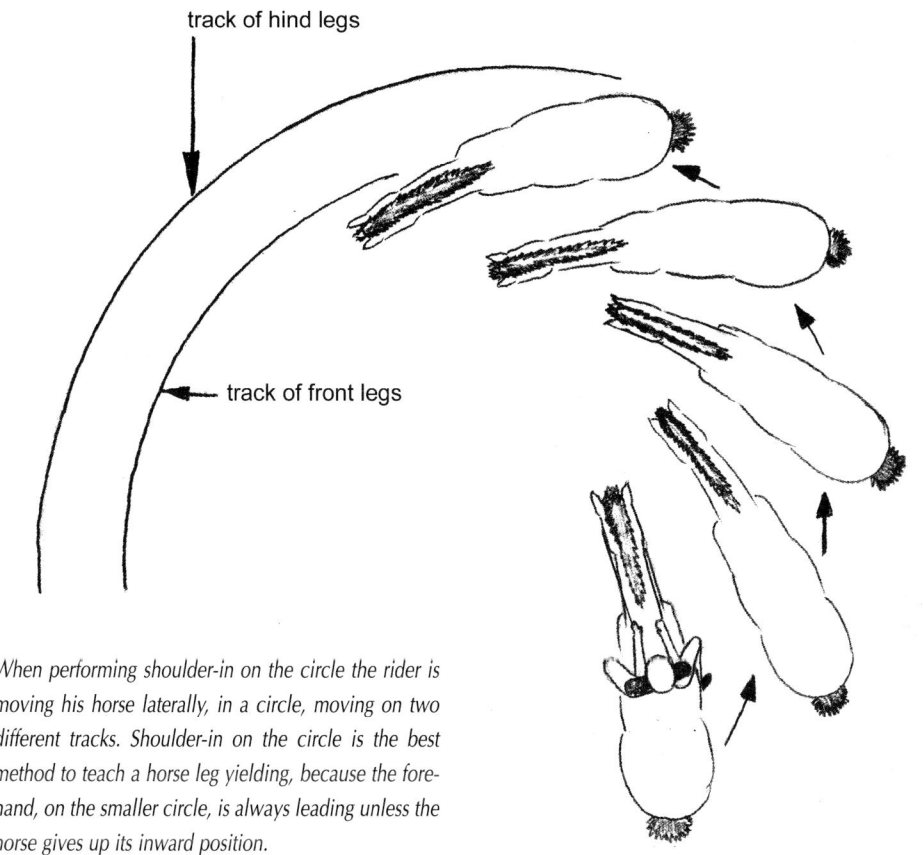

When performing shoulder-in on the circle the rider is moving his horse laterally, in a circle, moving on two different tracks. Shoulder-in on the circle is the best method to teach a horse leg yielding, because the forehand, on the smaller circle, is always leading unless the horse gives up its inward position.

movement. The last two steps of the turn, with the track opening up in front of the horse, will prove the most difficult, as the whip signal can now easily be interpreted as an aid to go forward and the half halts may not get through. It is much easier, for both horse and rider, if a skilled assistant or an instructor can offer some assistance from the ground. In advanced training, turns on the forehand will generally be executed in the middle of the sand-school.

The horse learns leg yielding

When working from the middle of the arena, the turn on the forehand can now be developed into leg yielding. The rider's inside leg still applies vibrant pressure on the girth, as in the turn on the forehand, but the rein aids no longer restrict the horse's forward movement. After one or two sideways steps, the horse will stretch forward. (If not, the forward impulsion in the turn on the forehand was not strong enough). The rider must now carefully contain this forward movement with the reins, just allowing the forehand to turn in a smaller circle than the quarters. By increasing this movement into the shoulder-in it can gradually be extended until the horse is working in a circle, fore and hindlegs on different tracks. Ultimately it is possible to move the horse smoothly into a forward/sideways action – the half-pass (which is also called 'counter-change of hands' when executed from the track diagonally to the centre line and then back to the track again) – where it is crucial that the shoulders are always slightly in advance of the hindquarters. The advantage of this teaching method is that having previously practised shoulder-in in a circle, the correct position of the horse is almost guaranteed, unless it gives up its inward position.

We cannot endorse a form of leg yielding where the horse is positioned facing the boards or a fence and is expected to move sideways. The horse has no other choice than to move sideways, even if the aids or the positioning are wrong or missing completely. In the end, this exercise will degenerate into some form of disciplinary action.

The horse learns the rein back

The horse will be introduced to the rein back during groundwork sessions, wearing a head collar and chain. The trainer positions the horse parallel to the boards on the first track and stands, facing towards the horse's tail, slightly in front of its shoulder. He gives a slight signal with the chain, uses a firm "Back" as a voice aid, and taps the horse lightly on the chest or the forelegs.

To begin with, the trainer should be satisfied with just one backward

To teach a horse the rein back, the trainer positions the horse parallel to the boards on the track and stands, facing the tail, slightly in front of its shoulder. He gives a slight signal with the chain, uses a firm "Back" as a voice aid, and taps the horse lightly on its chest or forelegs with a schooling whip.

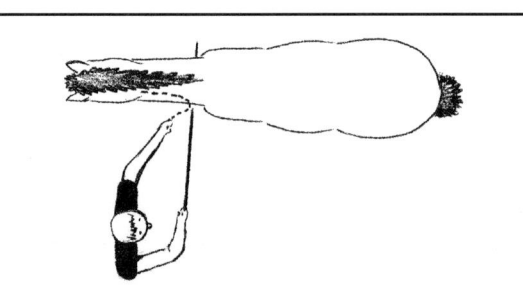

step. If the horse has problems with the rein back, it is important to lead it forward between each attempt. A horse that gets tighter and tighter with every step back makes the exercise more and more difficult for itself and the trainer may experience resistance. Every successful step backwards should be rewarded with a brief break, until the horse has finally learned to rein back fluently for several steps. When the horse has learned this lesson during groundwork, the rider can then proceed in the same fashion as in teaching turns on the forehand. Here too, an assistant is going to make life much easier.

The horse learns the turn on the haunches (half pirouette)

Teaching the turn on the haunches can only be attempted after the horse has learned to accept lateral leg aids on the girth, as well as behind the girth (leg yielding, position for cantering). The rider starts by practising short about-turns, where the hindlegs can initially move in a smaller circle until the horse moves in a minimal half circle, hindlegs stepping forward/sideways at the same time, almost on the spot, while the forehand moves around the quarters. The advantage of this approach is that the forward impulsion is maintained.

Natural Crookedness

If it has not happened before, then certainly by the time the rider is practising riding bends, he will come to a point when he asks himself why the horse is turning more smoothly on one side than the other.

The simple reason is that the majority of horses are naturally slightly crooked or asymmetrical, i.e. one hindleg turns out to be stronger and more dextrous than the other. It is the same in humans; some are left and some are right handed. Even a football player prefers to kick the ball with one particular foot, and it takes lots of hard work and talent to build up the strength in both legs.

The crooked horse places one hindleg further underneath its body than the other one, effectively placing this hindleg between the tracks of the forelegs. This stronger hindleg pushes powerfully against the shoulder on the same side, throwing it off balance. This crookedness can often be seen in dogs as well.

What the rider feels
This is how the rider can tell the horse is not straight: on the stiff side, the horse appears to resist both rein and leg. On the soft side, the horse

SVARTUR STIFF ON LEFT SIDE

50 Natural crookedness

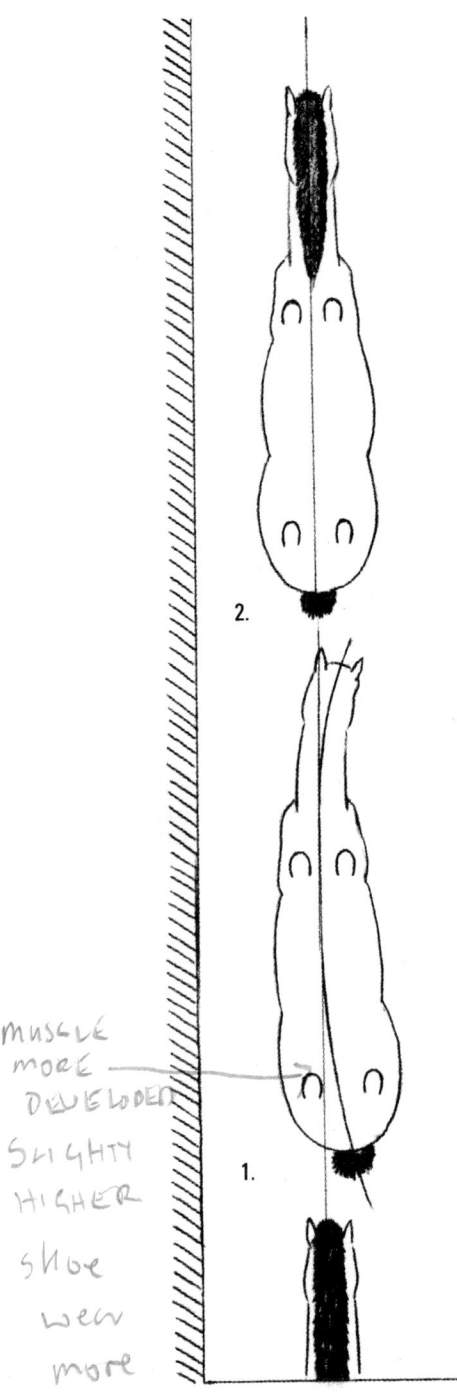

muscle
more
developed
slightly
higher
shoe
wear
more

feels hollow and will have a natural slight bend in that direction, making positioning to that side much easier. Some riders may have noticed in the past that when riding on one particular side (stiff side is outside) in a dressage arena or in the sandschool, they were forever hitting the boards with the stirrup, but this never happened when riding on the other rein (soft side is outside).

Consequences for the rider
If the rider doesn't want to make life more difficult for himself and his horse, if he wants the horse to become supple so that he can sit properly, then he has to learn to deal with this natural crookedness. A crooked horse will not allow the rider to sit properly in the saddle. This is because the back muscles on the stiff side are more developed and he will sit slightly higher on this side. If the rider decides to ignore the fact that the horse is not straight and sits unevenly in the saddle when applying driving aids, he will inadvertently cause the stronger hindleg to become stronger still.

Natural crookedness: every horse is naturally more adroit at using one hindleg than the other. It is left or right handed as humans are.
The horse places its more agile, stronger hindleg further underneath its body than the other one (1). To achieve suppleness, the horse's natural crookedness has to be corrected with every ride. The horse needs to be straightened. (2)

This will invariably result in the horse becoming stiffer and stiffer.

Many riders approach this problem by concentrating their efforts entirely on the stiff side, by a one-sided increase in the use of rein and leg and, if the horse is stiff on the right side, riding lots of right circles. Unfortunately, this could make the crookedness even worse. We have learned that half halts result in increased engagement of the hindleg on the same side. If, in order to soften the stiff side, the rider increasingly works on it using half halts as preparation, he is continuing to train the already stronger hindleg and the horse will become even stiffer on that side in the process.

Correction of natural crookedness
These examples have shown us that it is futile for the rider to try to 'soften' a horse's stiff side. The correct approach is to try to 'persuade' the horse to stretch for the bit on the hollow side. The rider must use his seat aids (weight and pelvis) to push the horse forward into the inner, softer rein, asking the horse for a stronger bit contact on the hollow side. If that is accepted, the stiff side will gradually soften by itself.

This shows us that the rider, no matter whether he is riding turns, or straight lines (where the natural crookedness is not quite as obvious), has to concentrate on keeping his horse straight all the time. In curved and in straight lines alike, he must always position his horse so that it can relax its back muscles. One option is to bend the horse to the right, if right is the stiff side. The inside rein indicates a slight bend to the right, the inside leg is applied on the girth, weight is on the inside seat bone and the pelvis is engaged on the inside. This inside positioning is rather difficult to obtain, as the rider really wants to get away from the inside rein. He wants to convince the horse to accept the outside rein. Co-ordination is very often a problem here for less experienced riders who often find themselves in a situation where they actually begin to fight the horse.

This is where the other option might be useful – Trying to soften the horse's stiff side with a counter bend. The rider now bends his horse to the outside (inside is the centre of the arena) and effectively reverses his swivel seat: his outside leg is applied on the girth, his inside leg, behind the girth, contains the bend. His weight is on his outer seat bone and his outside hip is pushed forward, engaging the pelvis. The rider tries to get the horse to make contact with the outside rein, at the same time trying to avoid any pressure on the inside rein. If, as a result of this, the horse's stiffness seems to shift from side to side, working stiffly on one day to the right and the next day to the left, this is a sign that the rider is on the right track.

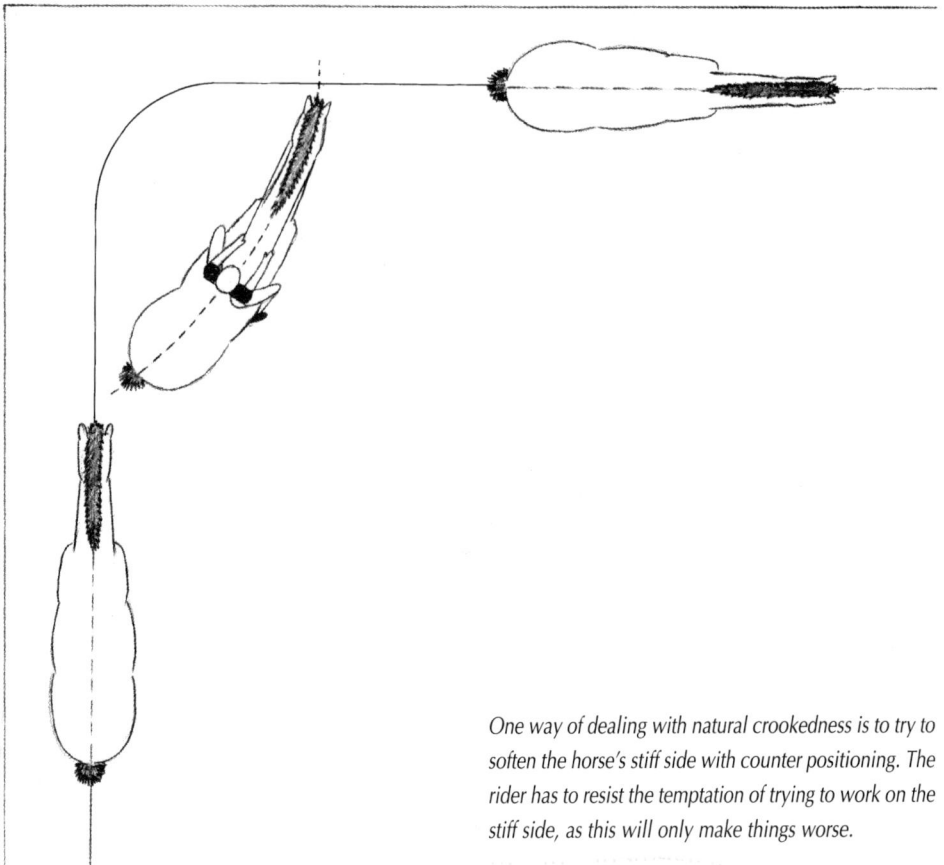

One way of dealing with natural crookedness is to try to soften the horse's stiff side with counter positioning. The rider has to resist the temptation of trying to work on the stiff side, as this will only make things worse.

Frequent changes of gaits and tempi are also very beneficial, because the hindlegs are encouraged to move forward more freely and to take more weight. When tense horses perform lateral or diagonal movements, their natural crookedness sometimes seems to change from side to side, suggesting there could be other ways of combating natural crookedness.

The rider has reached his goal if the horse accepts the same bit contact on either side of its mouth, both in bends and in straight lines. The horse's back muscles are relaxed and its natural crookedness has been eliminated at least for this lesson. Dealing with natural crookedness requires a great deal of knowledge and skill on the part of the rider. He has to work on it during every warm-up session before a ride and the problem has to be addressed again and again, whenever the horse enters a new stage of training.

Self-carriage of the Horse

It is safe to say that in the Icelandic Horse, self-carriage is at its most elevated form in the tölt and that is why the four-beat is in the centre of our "gait map" (see the section on Gaits). Self-carriage is a very important criteria when it comes to judging a ridden horse, so important in fact that many trainers cannot resist forcing the horse into this desired outline. They are deceiving themselves and leading their audience to believe that the horse is far more advanced than it actually is. It is true that the horse's self-carriage improves the more its training progresses. Horses will look proud, more expressive and their gaits will become more elevated, their performances poetry in motion. All this is the result of collection, achieved by greater engagement of the hindquarters, enabling the horse to move lightly and easily.

Self-carriage and Gait Distribution

Self-carriage is in itself an important objective, but especially so when it comes to riding the Icelandic Horse. The natural predisposition of the horse depends so much on the distribution of the gaits, which is reflected in its basic conformation. For example, in a horse that favours trot, you will find that the hindlegs – that's where good self-carriage starts – will move far more underneath the body than in a horse that favours pace. This means that the latter type of horse has to be trained much more to strengthen its hindquarters. Only when it is able to support the whole body can some form of collection be achieved and with it the start of good self-carriage.

We can safely say that five-gaited horses will, at first, need a lot more speed to balance themselves (that means balancing the combined weight of rider and horse). As soon as the hindquarters can take the weight, there is a marked improvement in the manoeuvrability and suppleness of the horse.

This example should make things a little clearer: many five-gaited horses present the rider with problems during canter training when asked to canter around the corner of a arena. They are on the forehand, have a tendency to break into pace, tense up and the rider can no longer sit properly. Because these horses have problems bending, they go so stiffly and deeply into the corner that even the most obedient of horses will end up inadvertently jumping over boundaries.

The difficulty of balancing the combined weight of horse and rider causes them to drift towards the outside and only a jump over the fence saves them from falling. In utter desperation, some horses resort to a disunited canter to try to get the support of the other hindleg.

Negative Flow

If the rider now attempts to solve the problem by trying to force the horse's neck up when it goes too far into the corner, he will invariably fail. By shortening the horse's frame in this way, the centre of gravity is admittedly moved further back towards the hindlegs, but the horse stays low in the shoulder and tightens its back. The body is still in the same outline as before and

A horse will only show impressive, proud, elevated and balanced self-carriage when it is relaxed and supple with actively engaged hindquarters. If the rider is not able to balance his horse, it will drop its shoulders and stay rigid in the back. As soon as the front comes up, the centre of gravity (X) moves backwards, no matter whether the horse's nose is low or its head and neck are raised.

Self-carriage of the horse 55

Stiff horses generally have a tendency towards negative flow: for instance, the stiff trotter that wasn't schooled properly in tölt and is tolted via rein aids alone. Its self carriage is wrong, its head moves towards the rider and the underside of its neck is pushed out. Shoulders stay low, hindquarters and croup are high. The horse's body is sloping downhill.

the rider has the feeling that he is constantly riding downhill. There is a dip in front of the saddle and no shoulder movement can be detected. The horse is simply not letting the rider sit and he almost hovers above the horse. We will call this sensation 'negative flow'. Stiff horses generally have a tendency towards negative flow. The perfect example is a four-gaiter with a preference for trot, whose tölt training has been forceful and mainly concentrated on the use of the reins.

This horse's head carriage has been achieved by simply pulling its head up. The head is lifted high towards the rider, the muscles of the lower neck are pushed forward and, in extreme cases, the highest point of the head is the nostrils. The shoulder is dropped, the back is tight with the croup is the highest point. The horse seems to slope downhill.

Positive Flow

For a lot of horses, this negative flow can only be changed into a positive one with the help of speed. If they are going quite fast, they stretch their whole body and self-carriage improves. The back becomes long and supple, the power of the hindquarters moves well underneath the horse and takes its shoulders

Self-carriage of the horse

The rider can change the self-carriage of his horse towards positive flow (engaged quarters, low croup, relaxed back muscles, raised shoulders) by simply 'playing' with the speed. He rides his horse forward and reduces the speed only as much as necessary to maintain positive flow.

higher. A skilful trainer can therefore improve the self-carriage of this type of horse by simply 'playing' with speed. In practice, this means he will ride the horse well forward and then take the speed back only gradually, never breaking the positive flow. The goal is to slow the tempo right down without losing the outline. Every rider should basically start his work at the point where the horse is offering this positive flow naturally (engaged quarters, soft back, high shoulders). He must therefore try to create situations where the horse is 'letting him sit', where he can feel the free shoulder movement in front of the saddle because the horse's back is so low and supple. This is a thrilling feeling that has been described by many as 'dancing'. To achieve this with high spirited or nervous horses, it has proved to be beneficial to ride in unknown terrain. Because the horse will be on its toes, trying to look at everything, the rider is in a good

A Gæðingur. The horse lets the rider sit properly. The rider can feel the shoulder movement. The horse's back swings so low that many riders have described this feeling as 'dancing'. The more the rider's driving aids come through, the more collection is achieved, and the horse will move even more impressively and become more comfortable in the process.

Self-carriage of the horse 57

3.

4.

position to apply forward driving aids. Still affected by their surroundings, horses will react with even more elevated movements, and have a positive flow with supple back and shoulder movements.

If a rider wants to experience what a trotting horse feels like in positive flow, he should try sitting trot over cavalletti.

But it is not only playing with the faster gaits that enables horses to achieve positive flow. Horses with a good walk can be taught to walk even faster. If the rider is experiencing a break into negative flow, he has to take his horse back with half halts and rebalance before trying again. In this way, he will gradually gain more and more speed within the positive flow.

One thing the trainer should keep in the back of his mind at all times is that 'correct' self-carriage differs from horse to horse. Depending on conformation and gait distribution, a higher or lower position of head and neck will be necessary. Training can only be considered right when positive flow is either improved or maintained. The rider can generally tell by judging how comfortably he is sitting.

Gaits

In order for a rider to train a gaited horse, he needs, initially, to get away from the theory of clearly divided gaits. The first step is to perceive the natural abilities of his horse as a skill that enables the horse to change, more or less fluently, from a lateral to a diagonal way of moving and vice versa. Riders who have had the opportunity to watch five-gaited foals in the field will confirm that they rarely stay in one particular gait for long. They slip smoothly from pace to a pacey tölt and sometimes into a trot-tölt or a trot. They have no problems changing from a four-beat canter into pace or tölt or the other way around.

It is possible to draw up a "gait map" for the Icelandic Horse, based on the way all these natural movements are connected.

If a trainer wants a supple horse that is comfortable in all gaits and which smoothly accepts the rider's aids regardless of whether it is in trot, tölt, canter, pace or walk, then he has to preserve the natural gait variations. Only if a horse's back muscles are evenly developed through training, both laterally and

Gaits

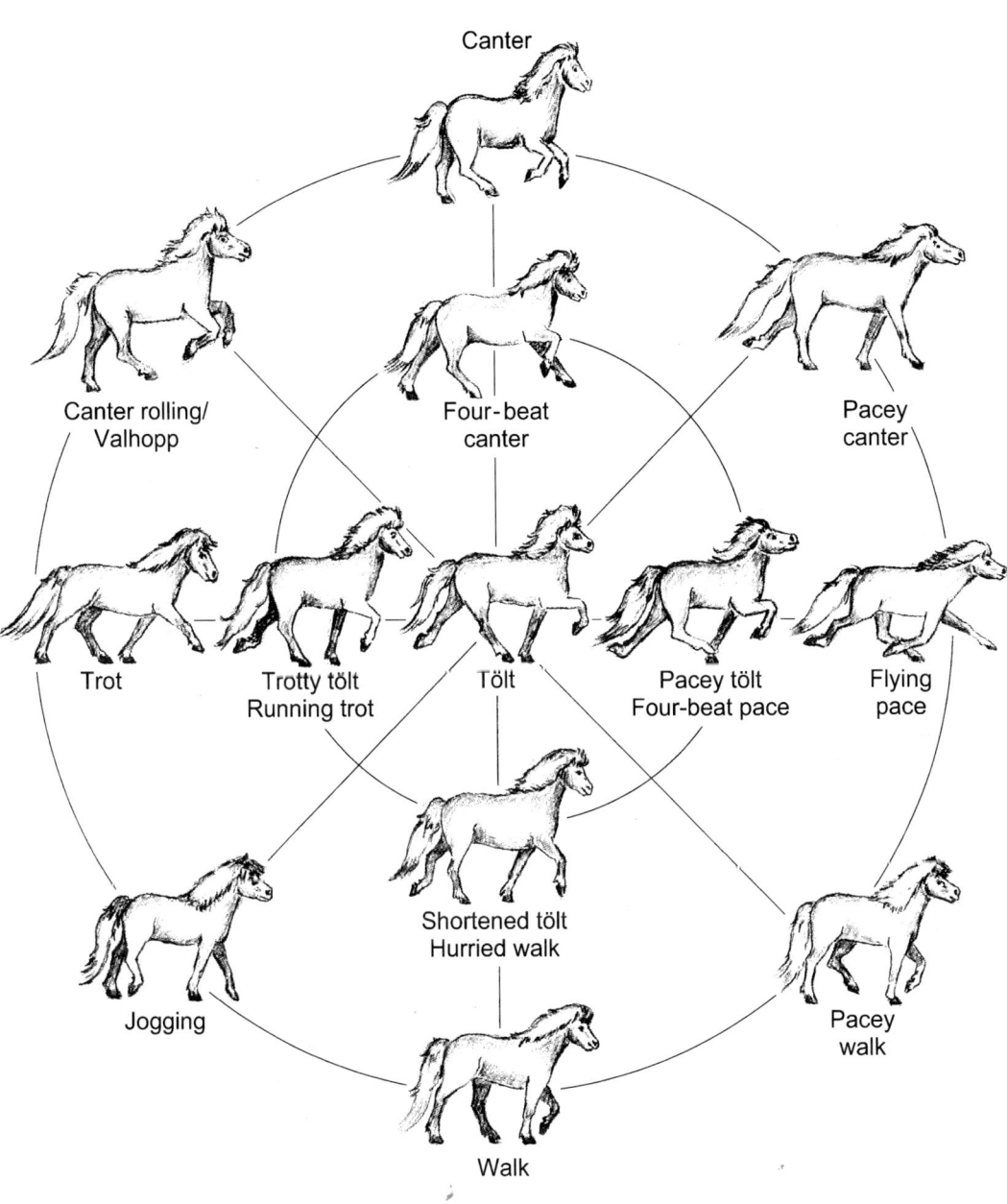

The 'gait map': Tölt is at the centre because it is in tölt that the horse shows the most sublime natural self-carriage. The rider should be able to change from tölt into trot, pace, canter or walk by simply letting the horse stretch out. He should ideally be able to take the horse from any gait harmoniously back into tölt, the clear four-beat.

diagonally, will it be prevented from developing a preference in either direction. Executing a smooth transition from all gaits into tölt, the four-beat, is the rider's ultimate goal.

The goal: four-beat

After the horse's basic training has been completed, the rider should, at first, only move within the inner circle of the gait map and not approach the outer circle until special training is called for. We should therefore focus our prime attention on the tölt, the gait where the horse naturally carries itself most majestically. A trainer who is concentrating principally on teaching the basic gaits or the pace is actually moving further and further away from the centre (goal: four-beat) and, as a result, will create problems later for his horse when he asks for a supple tölt. Let us take, for example, a horse that has been exclusively trained in trot, i.e. a two-beat. From here, it will only be able to switch into a tense and stiff pace, because, if you refer to our chart, the tölt has been completely omitted. The horse has changed from a supposedly 'super trot' directly into a pacey tölt. It might even, with a sigh of relief, 'dive' from the tense pacey tölt back into trot, and speed away with impressive action. A horse that has been trained in trot and is already inclined towards the two-beat will never achieve more than a choppy tölt, executed with dropped shoulders and a raised neck. It will always keep a tense high head carriage, because it is unable to progress beyond the four-beat, in a stretching movement, into a pacey tölt.

Only if the rider succeeds in continually moving his horse back towards the centre of the gait map will he experience a comfortable ride and be able to effectively apply seat and leg aids. This means he has to be able to slip the horse smoothly from a two or three-beat into a four-beat, or go from pace or canter gradually back to tölt, just by applying half halts. Approaching the outer limits (the outer circle of the map) should only be attempted by the rider when he is sure that he can find his way back to centre (the four-beat) without problems.

The diagonal movement in trot creates a wave-like up and down action through the horse's back and tail. This sets the rhythm for the rider's hip movements, either swinging passively or pushing forward for a stronger engagement of the pelvis.

When the horse favours a lateral, rhythmic up and down movement of its back stops. The movement topples sideways and alternately pulls the rider's left and right hip forward.

The rider cannot sit (or only with great difficulty). He will bring his seat further back, hunch his shoulders and push his legs towards the front. An active pelvic aid is no longer possible.

Gaits 61

Back aids

It is quite obvious to the observer that as soon as a horse, fixed in a lateral movement, slips into negative flow, the rider cannot get through to it with his seat and legs. This can be explained as follows: if the horse is in trot, a fast trot-tölt, or in tölt, the diagonally moving legs are creating a wave-like up and down movement through the horse's back and tail. This sets the rhythm for the rider's hip movements, either swinging passively or pushing forward with a stronger engagement of the pelvis. If, on the other hand, the horse is in a lateral gait, the rhythmic up and down movement of its back stops and the rider's left and right hips are alternately pulled forward. To swing alternate hips forward deliberately and rhythmically at such speed is anatomically almost impossible for the rider. Harmony of staying with the movement and at the same time any chance of applying seat aids, is lost. The rider will bring his seat further back to try to avoid the movement and, in doing so, hunch his shoulders and push his legs towards the front, effectively bracing himself against the stirrups in order to keep his seat still. Also typical in a rider on a laterally moving horse is the fact that his forward positioned legs now swing sideways, since it is almost impossible to apply leg aids on the girth of a horse with pacey action. Now we find ourselves in a vicious circle. Without correctly positioned legs, it is impossible to use the back actively.

To keep the horse's options open for all variations of the gaits and to be able to proceed smoothly from the outer circle of the gait map towards the inner, (the clear four-beat), the rider has to employ half halts to vary the degree of collection. Here is a reminder: every half halt has to be followed by giving with the reins, every attempt at collection is followed by a period of stretching and relaxing, giving the horse the opportunity to find its balance.

Many a rider will have experienced the amazing effect of this to-ing and fro-ing, especially if he owns a horse with a tendency to tense up laterally, one that normally goes flat and uncollected and does not accept any driving aids. This type of horse can really have its moments when ridden in unfamiliar country. It is distracted by the novelty of its surroundings and when going round a corner, for example, can really be on its toes. Now its self-carriage will become more elevated, it is collected, the quarters are engaged and the rider can finally get through with his driving aids, achieving a clear beat tölt.

This great feeling which the rider now experiences with his inspired horse is the direct result of his mount lowering and swinging its back. The motion of the 'wave' is taking the rider deep down 'into' the horse, where he can feel the shoulder movement in front of the saddle. The quarters are low and engaged: the horse's whole body seems to slope uphill. This produces, as any audience will confirm, a far better picture than a horse that simply has a high leg action. A horse that pulls its legs up can admittedly have 'action', but with dropped shoulders it is still 'sloping downhill' – a feeling the observer cannot appreciate if he hasn't experienced it for himself from the saddle.

On the bit

If the horse's back movements are supple and their flow is bringing the hindquarters smoothly underneath its body in every situation, then we can safely say that the rest of the horse's self-carriage is good as well. And that brings us neatly to the much disputed topic: 'being on the bit'. Riders often misinterpret this expression as 'being in a dressage-like outline'. If a horse is 'taking it's stupid head down', as so many rather unkindly request of their charges, many riders now think that it must be on the bit as well. This is the reason why such riders will start very early in their training to pull the horse's head down, with either an extremely low hand, or the use of side reins. The expression 'on the bit' has basically very little to do with the horse's self-carriage. It does, however, make a statement about the flow of movement that the engaged quarters transport via a supple back into the direction of the bit. This results in a horse whose whole body is part of one graceful harmonic motion, giving the rider the most comfortable of rides. The equation goes like this: correct function of quarters + correct function of back = self-carriage.

From this we can deduce two things. The first is that, depending on the stage of its training, the horse will be on the bit, but still shows different types of self-carriage. In early stages of training, the horse's head might either be more upright or rather low in comparison with the later stages of training. And the second is that a horse can be on the bit even in tölt or pace, gaits that are definitely not ridden in the classical dressage type outline, by simply adopting the self-carriage typical of the gait. The crucial factor is a supple, swinging back, which transports the movement over the poll into the horse's mouth and back again.

Playing with the gaits

A good trainer can take advantage of playing with the horse's gaits, for instance, if the horse tölts with a relatively high self-carriage and is getting a little too tight. If he feels the horse needs to stretch its back, he can always slip it into trot, canter or pace, all gaits where a less collected outline is required. If the horse gets too flat, the outline too extended, the trainer will bring it back into tölt by applying half halts. In order to make this 'way back' as light and easy as possible, it is important not to expect these half halts to produce tölt immediately, which would be a sign of having created excessive tension. To be able to perform a smooth transition, the trainer should keep the horse slightly collected when riding trot, canter and pace. He should not allow too much stretching, in order to stay as close as possible to the four-beat. It has therefore proved beneficial at this stage of training to allow the horse to trot the Icelandic way, i.e. in a flatter movement with a slightly higher neck and head carriage. The horse's back will stay more relaxed and the dreaded phenomenon of getting locked into one of the two extremes – lateral or diagonal preference – will not occur. The horse has to understand these transitions and be able to slip effortlessly from one gait variation into another. Only then should the trainer move the gait training further away from the four-beat.

The trainer can take advantage of the horse's relatively high self-carriage in tölt. If he needs a more extended outline because the horse gets too tight, he can always slip it into trot, canter or pace - all gaits where the horse has to stretch. If the horse gets too flat, he brings it back into tölt by applying half halts. Playing with the gaits will bring the horse into positive flow.

At this stage of training it is a good idea to let the horse trot with a higher (Icelandic style) self-carriage (above). In this way one can move easily between trot and tölt without the horse locking its back.

Collecting the horse

By now the rider has smoothly balanced his horse's gaits, within the boundaries of the gait map, depending on its natural gait distribution. This means he can slip effortlessly from a slightly tense tölt towards pace, until the desired outline is found, and the transitions between the gaits are light and easy. Let's turn to the next step in gait training, the fine-tuning of a horse's action, working on the accentuation of the movement, again, in total harmony with the horse. As always, it is going to be important to find the right balance between collection and lengthening exercises. Delicate half halts will result in engaging the hindquarters more and more and, by giving with the reins, some of the created impulsion can be released if the rider wants to avoid the horse getting too tight. By skilfully giving and taking, rider and horse will finally approach the point of perfect collection. This is the stage where

Gaits

'On the bit' is often misinterpreted as meaning a dressage type outline. It actually means that the horse, independent of its outline, carries the impulsion created by its engaged quarters via a supple back towards the bit. This means that horses can be on the bit in tölt as well as in flying pace, as Karly Zingsheim with Dama frá Hólum or Dorte Rassmussen with Blossi prove.

the horse will ultimately give a ride like a dream horse, a Gæðingur.

Artificial manipulation

Some trainers just cannot resist the temptation of going for the clear four-beat straight away, without making the horse supple first. That is when they turn to artificial manipulation. With the assistance of weights and other means, the emphasis of training is entirely directed to the action of the forelegs. This does achieve a lifting of the shoulders, and it has a partial effect on the back muscles too, but energy created like this cannot flow through the whole body, and will definitely never reach the quarters where it is needed to create activity. The horse might now perform an audible four-beat with its legs, but the whole body is tense and still moves more in a pace-like fashion, making it impossible for the rider to sit. It might not be as uncomfortable as sitting on a stiff horse with dropped shoulders, but it is still a far cry from the feel a really supple horse gives. Horses that have been trained in this way are not able to co-ordinate their fore and hind legs in harmony, and the body is also out of tune with the movement of their legs. On top of that, the rider doesn't produce a performance (clear four-beat, high forehand action) in unison with his horse. He is actually forcing it into an unnatural and tense movement with these methods . This puts artificial manipulation firmly into the category of deception, which can easily be recognised even by a novice who has a little sense of harmony. Artificial manipulation should therefore be rejected.

Training for the Different Gaits

In order to be able to describe the different gaits, we had to sort through the endless variety of Icelandic Horses' talents and divide them into different types. Using these types as a starting point, we will show how, based on individual talents, they could lead towards a dream horse.

We will also make a distinction between the so-called 'free tempo' and the 'ridden tempo'. The tempo that a horse offers naturally within a given gait will be called 'free tempo'. This is the tempo we will conduct our training in, and also probably the tempo the majority of leisure riders will choose later on. The 'ridden tempo' will refer to the

Gaits

Artificial manipulation and the tölter: when concentrating on the front, the forehand has a high and wide action as if performing fast tölt. The quarters, if one ignores the front, seem to step in a working tempo. This horse is tight in its back and the rider can't sit. The rider tips backwards from the hips and hunches his shoulders. His legs slip forward.

The meaning of 'on the bit' has basically nothing to do with self-carriage of the horse. It only states that impulsion can flow from the quarters via the back to the reins. It means that a horse, depending on its stage of training, can be on the bit in many different outlines. On the other hand, a horse that is forced into a dressage-like outline is not on the bit, because it is in negative flow and the rider's aids cannot get through.

tempi that are expected from sport horses during competitions. Because the 'ridden tempo' only represents a natural progression from the 'free tempo', the latter, being the basis of our work, will obviously take up more room in this book.

We will also give riders practical tips on how to improve their horses in a certain gait, without meeting resistance. These tips can be especially useful for the leisure rider. Here, for instance, he will learn that it is better to trot a horse in heavy ground and not try to tölt, or that a pacey tölter is better when ridden forward at all times and that any attempts to tölt should be restricted to areas with a slight downhill inclination.

The main emphasis in our reflections on the training of the gaited horse is on tölt and pace, as there are already a good many competent instructors who have written excellent books on the training of walk, trot and canter. We will mention these basic gaits only in their relevance to gait training. One more thing. We have positioned every one of our horse 'types' within our circle gait map, marked with a small circle: arrows show the direction of development towards which this horse has to be trained. This basically means that if the arrow points towards the middle of the map, i.e. in the direction of tölt (four-beat), the horse has to be brought more onto the haunches with a higher elevation at the front. If the arrow points from the inside out, this shows the direction the horse's training has to follow.

Walk

Footfalls, seat and tempo
The walk is a four-beat gait with eight phases. The sequence in which the legs leave the ground is as follows: left hindleg, left foreleg, right hindleg, right foreleg.

Walk is ridden in the basic seat. The majority of leisure riders ride the walk entirely in free tempo. Competitions for Icelandic Horses, on the other hand, expect to see a medium walk with the horse on the bit (ridden walk). For aids to moving off in walk, please refer back to the chapter on the combined use of aids.

Natural predisposition
The Icelandic Horse normally has quite a good walk, but the natural predisposition of the horse can only be seen for sure if it moves in a light and relaxed manner. As there is little impulsion in walk, the rider has far less opportunity to influence the movement than in trot, tölt, canter or pace, and the choices available to improve the engagement of the quarters are limited.

On the other hand, the walk tells us a lot about the training of a horse. Lack of trust and dubious training methods, specifically in other gaits, can be detected in the walk when the horse doesn't move freely or is either fidgeting or 'creeping' behind the bit.

Any attempt by the rider to try to force a walking horse into a certain outline is generally followed by an immediate loss of rhythm.

Faults in walk and their correction
Faults in walk are, as already pointed out, mostly a result of the rider's errors in the training of other gaits. For this reason, and let us say this again, it is absolutely pointless to try to correct these problems in walk (for instance by riding through deep ground or over rails). Exercises like

Gaits – Trot

The walk tells us a lot about the training of a horse. Lack of trust and dubious training methods in other gaits have to be paid for in walk and can easily be detected in this gait, for instance, when the horse fidgets or 'creeps' behind the bit.

this will only bring short-term results because the basic problem has not been dealt with. If a horse is worked properly in all gaits, then the walk will be as good as the horse's natural talents allow it to be.

Trot

Footfalls, seat and tempo

The trot is a two-beat gait with four phases. The horse's legs leave the ground in diagonal pairs as follows: left hindleg and right foreleg; right hindleg and left foreleg. There is a moment of suspension in between. Trot can be ridden in the basic seat, the relief seat or the rider can post, i.e. sitting down on every second step. When riding rising trot, the rider should frequently change the diagonal, in order to develop the horse's hindlegs equally. If changing the diagonal is causing the horse to break the gait, it is better to ride trot in the relief seat or as sitting trot, instead of continuing to put increased weight on one hindleg.

Most leisure riders will allow their horses to trot mainly in free tempo, as it is the easiest gait for the horse to tackle rough terrain. (That too is the reason why most horses will trot over cavalletti). Working trot and medium trot will be asked for during Icelandic Horse competitions.

Natural predisposition and types
Icelandic Horses show basically two types of trot tendencies:

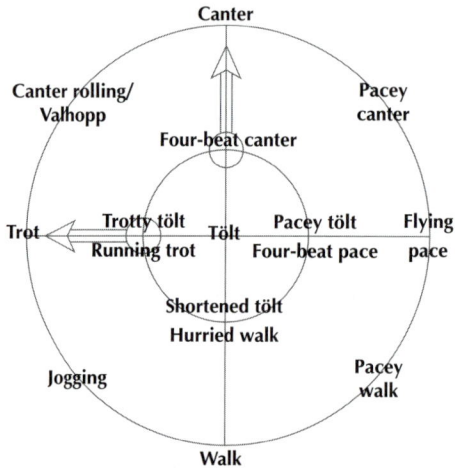

Gait: trot
Type: running trot

Type 1: The running trotter
Horses of this type do a very fast, almost four-beat, trot. Sometimes they cannot even trot properly, but show a tölt which tends towards trot. The training goal for such horses is to bring them closer to the two-beat.

The trainer can either start by letting the horse run beside a lead horse or, preferably, train the trot by loose-schooling in the arena. Both exercises develop the horse's muscles in the gait, but without the weight of a rider. At the same time tölt training should be continued. The trainer concentrates on achieving maximum suppleness. A horse that accepts half halts without tension will become more collected in the process. The more the quarters become engaged, the easier it will be for the horse to find trot. Gradually, the rider will allow the horse to stretch, but only to the point where a half halt can still produce enough collection to avoid the horse trotting with its weight on the forehand.

Type 2: The stiff trotter
a) Basic gaits only
This type of horse performs the trot in a true two-beat, often accompanied by impressive high action. However, because these horses are unable to execute a smooth transition into the four-beat, we still call them 'stiff', despite their good trot. In this context, even the Icelanders

Gaits – Trot   73

Supple movements and high self-carriage: the horse is trotting on the bit.

talk about 'crude movements'. Such horses must learn to trot with a higher head carriage, but still stay supple. That is why horses in Iceland are not generally trotted in a low and extended outline and why Icelanders never post. They stay close to the saddle, ready to apply seat aids to break the two-beat rhythm towards the tölt, and use a brief tugging rein aid (see chapter on bits) to keep the horse's nose forward and up.

b] Basic gaits and pace
This type of horse can hardly vary the speed of its trot, has a tendency to lean on the forehand and generally moves in a rather extended outline. It had to physically 'learn' the trot during its basic training. In these circumstances, trainers will try to improve the trot by asking for a higher self-carriage and riding lots of tempo transitions. This will, at the same time, act as a preparation for

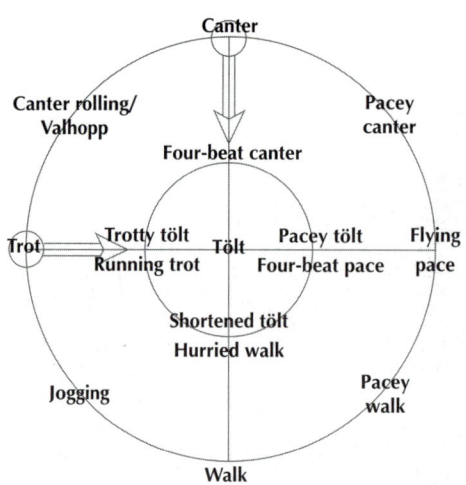

Gait: trot
Type: stiff trotter

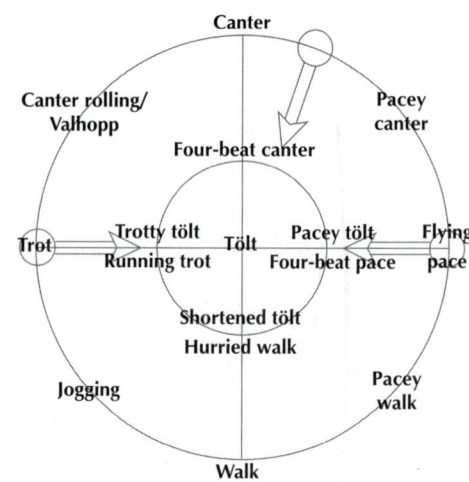

Gait: trot
Type: basic gaits and pace

tölt training (see tölt, the stiff tölter).

Tölt

Footfalls, seat and tempo
Tölt is a four-beat gait with eight phases. The sequence in which the legs leave the ground is as follows: left hindleg, left foreleg, right hindleg, right foreleg. One distinguishes between free tempo and ridden tempi (working, medium and extended tempo). The rider is generally in the basic seat position, but slight variations towards the relief seat are possible. For moving off in tölt, see chapter on the combined use of aids.

Natural predisposition and types
As a rule of thumb for working on the tölt, one could say that the less natural the tölt is, the more experienced the rider has to be and the longer the training will take. If one applies the rough criteria of types again, one can find quite different talents for tölt in the Icelandic Horse. The natural tölter will prefer, and offer, the tölt to all other gaits and changes easily into trot, or in the direction of trot, or into a four-beat canter. Then there is the tölter who is almost impossible to slip into trot and, with increasing speed, will come closer and closer to pace, both in type of movement and posture. Finally, we have the group of relatively stiff horses who only volunteer trot and pace, or sometimes exclusively one of the two (they do, of course, walk and canter).

Gaits – Tölt

Tölt, the gait that endeared the Icelandic Horse to leisure and competition riders, because a relaxed horse moving in harmony is very comfortable to ride.

The natural tölter

The easy natural tölter usually has a supple back and possesses the ideal self-carriage (positive flow), which allows the rider to further the horse's training in whichever direction he chooses (refer to the gait map). Most of the time, these tölters will need little intervention from the rider as long as they are allowed to choose their own tempo. After basic training, the rider will only need to work on the tölt to improve general suppleness, obedience and stamina. However, being a natural tölter doesn't mean that the horse is not able to perform in other gaits. Advanced training will include these other gaits as well, bringing the horse closer to the outer limits of the gait map. The last step is to perfect the ridden tempi, i.e. working, medium and fast tölt.

Problem: breaking the four-beat > canter-rolling
Canter-rolling in tölt, as this tendency

towards the canter is known, occurs quite often in the early stages when lungeing the natural tölter. Because their movements are so loose, they react to every bend by re-balancing and loosing the four-beat. Many of these horses will be spoiled even further when the ridden training begins, as the rider, in order to correct this rolling, constantly rides turns and bends, thus interrupting the natural flow of movement. A horse that was once a supple natural tölter very often ends up becoming stiff towards pace. It is therefore much better to ignore the rolling at first and proceed by preferably riding in a straight line, changing the rein often and attempting only shallow bends. The trainer has to follow this regime strictly until the horse accepts his aids precisely and is free from tension.

Problem: speed
Many natural tölters can only perform the gait very slowly and will break into a running canter as soon as the tempo increases. Their head carriage then becomes too high (tendency towards the 'valhopp', where neck and head are up, the forelegs canter, but the hindlegs 'run', maintaining a two-beat) and they often find it difficult to go forward smoothly.

If this problem was not resolved in the early stages of training by using a balancing rein (Equilonge), the rider is now faced with the task

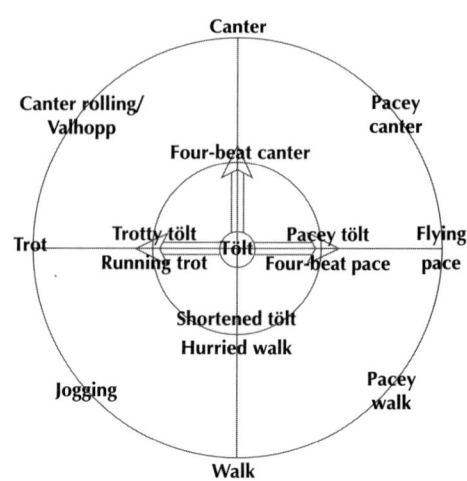

Gait: tölt
Type: the natural tölter

of creating enough impulsion to get the horse to accept the bit. The first phase of the half halt will see a passive hand that goes with the horse, encouraging it to stretch for the bit. The second phase, giving the reins for a brief moment, is slightly extended in order to get the horse into a longer outline. This type of horse often has similar problems when it comes to trotting. It only trots slowly and doesn't seem to go forward at all. It might prove beneficial for such horses to be galloped at speed for short distances, making sure that only a flexible rein contact is kept, almost encouraging them to lean slightly on the bit, and hoping, in this way, to extend their outline. As horses of this type are commonly not at all forward-going, they should be hacked out a lot, or ridden in a group to encourage their competitive spirit.

Type: The pacey tölter
Horses of this type are able to tölt loosely up to a medium tempo, even then showing a little tendency towards pace. Their extended outline reacts to any increase in tempo by moving closer and closer towards the two-beat. Pacey tölters already show a distinct lateral inclination at slow speeds, and the trainer has to concentrate on working on collection and getting these horses onto their haunches.

Problem: self-carriage
The skilled trainer will take every opportunity to get the horse to respond to his driving aids. This is best achieved when riding in surroundings where the horse is slightly distracted and likely to be a bit on its toes. Riding forward at speed is also a good exercise, whereas tight turns should be avoided, as horses' bodies are usually rather stiff when it comes to bending. Choosing a suitable route when out hacking is also help-

The pacey tölter will extend its outline more and more as tempo increases. The rider must generally aim to get through with his driving aids in order to activate the quarters. The hindlegs have to step under the body actively to take the weight and help balance the horse. A skilled trainer will also choose the right track, in this case slightly downhill, when out hacking and make it more difficult for the horse to leave the hindlegs behind. In this way the quarters have to engage more.

ful. Riding slightly downhill will make it more difficult for the horse to leave the hindlegs behind, so the quarters will engage more, and that in itself will improve the self carriage no end.

Problem: gait transitions
When trying to get the pacey tölter collected by using half halts, the rider must be very careful not to let the horse slip into negative flow, with a high croup, stiff back and dropped shoulders. It is also not a good idea to use canter for loosening exercises, as this is a gait that these horses are generally not very good at. As the rider gradually succeeds in teaching this type of horse to tölt with a higher self-carriage, while at the same time maintaining positive flow, its natural inclination will increasingly shift in the direction of trot, and will be followed by an improvement in tölt.

However, it is not wise to start the

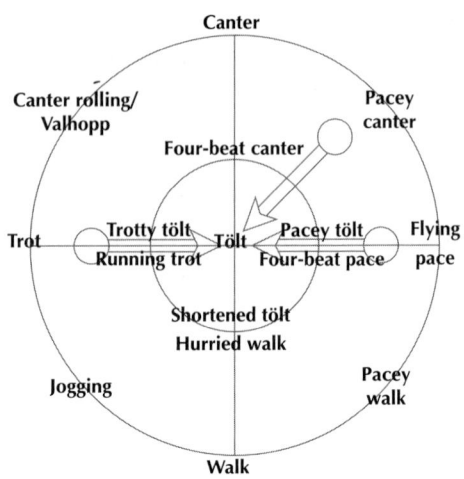

Gait: tölt
Type: the pacey tölter

training by working on the trot first, because this normally results in a sluggish trot that leaves the horse on the forehand. From this position, they will generally break into pace again. There is only one way: the pacey tölter has to be brought back onto the haunches by using half halts, and then, from a clear beat tölt, moved via a running trot into correct trot. As soon as it has reached the stage where it shows a tendency towards running trot, this type of horse will suddenly start to roll when asked to move uphill. This rolling, which is a breaking towards canter, can be used to advantage in tölt training, as a quiet canter will always result in the horse's shoulders being raised. Once the horse is in a four-beat canter, the rider can 'start work on the diagonal' and this will also move the pacey tölter a little closer towards trot. With continuous but sensitive transitions between tölt, pacey tölt and a collected four-beat canter, it is possible for the trainer to get his horse into a positive flow, and to move fluently into tölt and running trot.

In the beginning, it is advisable to practise these gait transitions riding uphill only. Later on, the rider can train on the flat until his horse accepts the half halts so easily that it

With continual transitions between tölt, pacey tölt and a collected four-beat canter, the trainer will get his horse into positive flow. From a four-beat canter the rider has the opportunity to 'start work on the diagonal' and move his pacey tölter a little closer towards trot – in the direction of the clear four-beat.

will move fluently from a four-beat canter into tölt without going onto the forehand.

Having come this far, the trainer can now concentrate on improving the riding of turns, as a supple tölt has been established and this will prevent negative flow from appearing again.

Type: The stiff tölter   TYR.

Stiff tölters have a strong tendency towards either a lateral or a diagonal movement, sometimes both. At first, it is almost impossible, or at least very difficult, to get this type of horse to tölt. It needs to learn to be extremely alert and sensitive in accepting basic aids, so that the trainer can guide it, with minute accuracy, fluently towards the four-beat.

This fact alone makes it clear that stiff types need much more time spent on training than supple ones. It also requires a horse that is eager to learn and willing to please and a sufficiently experienced and skilled trainer. Stiff types are uncomfortable for the rider, whether they lean towards trot or pace. On top of this, we often find them insensitive in the mouth, because their general stiffness blocks the flow of movement and they do not have the opportunity to stretch for the bit. The training must aim to produce a horse that is comfortable to ride and reacts sensibly to any rein aids.

Stiff tölters can be divided into two types, that should be ridden and trained as follows:

Horses that are stiff and trotty

If a stiff horse favours a trot, and with it diagonal movement, it should effortlessly master basic training. It will generally bend easily, which is an asset when riding turns. Problems normally start occurring when it needs to learn a different movement, like the four-beat, as this also requires more than average will.

→ learning the tölt:
   from walk to tölt

The safest way for the trainer to reach this goal is to proceed as follows:

Ride the horse in walk, taking short steps, and move it steadily towards pace. This pace-like walking

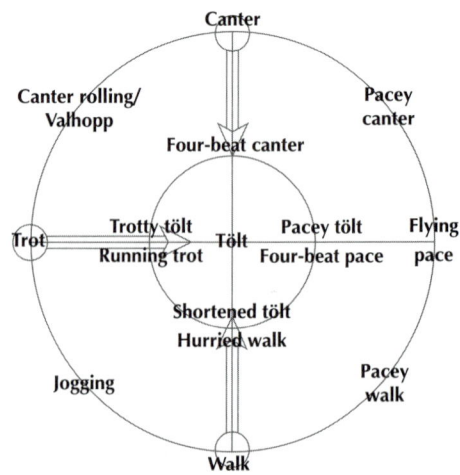

Gait: tölt
Type: stiff and trotty

Gaits – Tölt 81

Learning to tölt: the stiff trotter has learned to go forward in pacey action without rein contact. He has been taught to understand the lateral movement, to walk in an extended outline. Further training is now similar to the task that the trainer of a stiff five-gaiter faces: he moves the horse from trot and canter on one side of the gait map, and a pace like walk on the other side, more and more towards the centre of the gait map, the clear four-beat.

should now be gradually increased in tempo, but care must be taken that the horse stays 'pace-like' and doesn't break into a four-beat. At the moment when the rider begins to feel the typical wave-movement of a diagonally moving horse in his back (feels a bit like trot), he needs to

reduce the tempo again by applying half halts. This is a sign that the horse has not yet learned to move fluently and, without the half halt, would immediately topple back into a diagonal movement.

It is best to practise this pacey walk only for short distances, e.g. for a few meters, and only when the horse is full of energy and is raring to go. This is probably best achieved when riding last in a group, or on the way home from a hack (though not if the horse is tired). The trainer really needs to develop a thorough knowledge of the psyche of his horse in order to safeguard that the will for work is not lost. We are, after all, expecting the horse to understand that the meaning of the driving aids has suddenly changed and that they don't just mean 'go forward' anymore.

For this reason, it is vital to keep working on the horse's suppleness and obedience (turns on the forehand, leg yielding, rein back etc.) in between working on these 'tölt exercises'. The rider must also frequently allow his pupil to stretch out on a loose rein. It is also very important that the horse is given the opportunity for the odd carefree run. This is best provided without the weight of a rider, either on the lunge, loose schooling, or on a hack as a hand horse. The work from the shortened walk has served its purpose when the rider is able to ride his horse, at a working tempo, in a pace-like forward movement, and he knows his horse has learned the footfalls, how to move its back and the feel of lateral movement.

It is now able to perform a pace-like movement without being forced by rein aids, but there is still a long way to go before suppleness is achieved. At this stage of training there is still a danger that the horse gets stuck in trot or in an even stronger pace-like action, which will inevitably lead to increased tension and can result in what the Icelanders call Víxl*.

Further training should now be similar to that for the stiff five-gaiter: the trainer moves his horse from trot and canter on one side of the gait map, or from pacey tölt on the other, more and more towards the middle of the gait map; towards a clear four-beat.

In this way, even less experienced riders can start a horse's tölt training (under supervision of an instructor) as they have had enough time to fine tune their aids during the 'shortened walk' exercises.

→ using speed to teach tölt

There is a way to get horses tölting by using speed alone. However, the trainer should only follow this avenue when he feels that the horse is not too far away from the four-beat in the first place. This means that despite the horse only offering trot in the basic stages, it has sufficient natural tölt ability. A rider who wants to get his horse to tölt by means of speed has to be very skilful and precise with his rein aids, and must have a secure and effective seat in all situations.

---

*Víxl (also called mixing) can be described as follows:
The horse moves from the four-beat more and more towards a lateral two-beat, but still retains the normal sequence of footfalls: hind first, then front. Now the horse stiffens, is in a clear two-beat, and puts down its hind and forelegs on the same side simultaneously. At this point, it becomes even more tense, to the point that the foreleg will be put down before the hindleg. It becomes even tenser, until the hindleg is about to track the foreleg, which hasn't yet been lifted. As horses don't tread on their own feet, it will now miss a step with the hindleg, waiting for the foreleg to give way and simultaneously rearranging the other legs, which will leave it in either trot or clean tölt. Víxl is always the result of negative flow, or more accurately, its strongest form.

The horse needs to be ridden on a slight downhill track, its speed just a little higher than normal trotting tempo, as any gait performed at racing speed and any excessive demands put on a horse will automatically lead to the four-beat. Then, from high speed, the tempo is gradually decreased. The rider must try to use his hands as little as possible and rely on his driving aids to achieve collection, otherwise he will end up with a horse that is too high up in front. If he fails, the horse will drop its shoulders into negative flow. Again, when doing these exercises, do not forget to work on the horse's obedience at the same time.

The trainer should also be aware that every attempt of the horse to roll, no matter what the tempo, will bring the horse from a trot towards a four-beat, affecting each diagonal. When a stage of training has been reached where the horse has moved on from being on a pure diagonal, it can be beneficial to take advantage of the horse's rolling by changing between a left and a right roll. But even when using speed to get the tölt, the horse can suddenly become too pacey and consequently has to be ridden like a stiff five-gaiter. Indeed, both methods can suddenly result in the horse not trotting at all for a while, especially in a nervous type.

Horses that are stiff and pacey
Stiff horses with a strong tendency towards the lateral, i.e. the pace, often find it very hard during basic training, as they can only bend with great difficulty and are generally not very mobile. Further work is going to be even more difficult if these pacers did not learn to trot during their basic schooling.

→ Problem: finding trot and canter
Because these horses are occasionally so far away from any diagonal movement, it is quite acceptable for them to trot on the forehand, just to get them used to some different rhythm of movement. However, it is sometimes a physical impossibility for the muscular system of their backs to produce a lateral action. But if the basic schooling has been done properly, most stiff pacers will have learned to trot on the forehand. In really difficult and exceptional

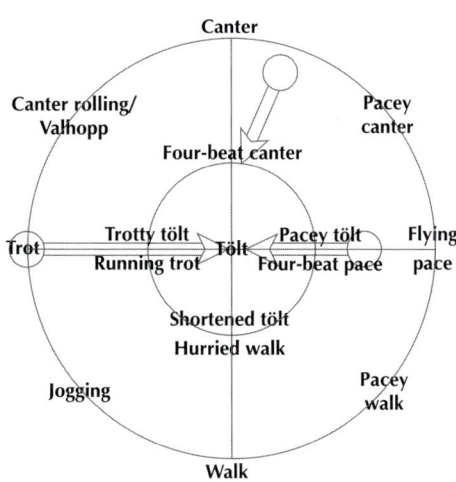

Gait: tölt
Type: stiff and pacey

A horse that is stiff and pacey is so low in front that it cannot balance itself. A rigid back will not let the movement flow through, the quarters are not engaged, and the rider cannot sit.

cases, one might be successful in getting these horses to trot by forcing them from a slow pace into Víxl, and then, hopefully, continuing in trot.

The next phase in the schooling programme of the stiff pacer is to learn to change tempi in trot. We will generally encourage a high head carriage (it can't be too high as long as the horse doesn't lean on the bit) to give the trot a slight tendency towards the four-beat.

In canter as well, starting on straight tracks and later on bends, it is advisable to ride these horses with a high head carriage (again, it can't be too high, otherwise the horse will break into pace). This should teach them to 'run' behind and stay low with the quarters. On top of this, the rider should practice a lot of transitions from trot to canter and back again and should attempt to slow the transition phases as much as possible. Extending the time that the hindlegs are actively stepping will help the horse to become increasingly fluent in the changes. The main aim of this trot and canter work is to lift the forehand, to bring the quarters more underneath the centre of gravity and to achieve a better self-carriage within the positive flow. To achieve this, the rider should select slight uphill tracks and softer ground.

→ From walk to tölt

The rider can also approach his

goal, the four-beat, from the other side, by riding the horse in an energetic walk, with active quarters. He increases the tempo but immediately applies half halts when the wave movement of the back stops. Gradually, the gap between walk tempo and canter-trot tempo is closed. Trot and canter will come closer to the four-beat until tölt is reached and, from there, the horse can be taken back fluently into walk, without losing the wave movement of the back.

→ Playing with the gaits

The rider has to work very carefully on transitions. From an initial fast trot, the horse is slowed down by a combination of driving seat, leg aids and containing rein aids, until it changes fluently into tölt. By keeping the horse high in front, the tempo can be reduced to walk. Alternatively, the rider can gradually release the impulsion to create more speed, or a transition into trot and allow the horse into a more extended outline. In these exercises, where the rider starts by asking his horse for speed, one has to accept a certain loss of high self carriage. However, the goal is to achieve upward transitions, or a change into trot, without letting the horse become lower in the front and with an ever-increasing aim for true collection.

→ Giving the horse a change

Some trainers find it beneficial to occasionally take the stiff five-gaiter out for a hack and allow it to piggy-pace. The idea is to make the horse realise that it is not always hard work when it is ridden. However, the trainer is running the risk of confusing his pupil, as the aim of schooling is to eradicate piggy-pace, because it brings the horse into negative flow. We think that groundwork, lungeing or taking the novice as a hand horse are more valuable in giving the horse a break.

Ridden tempi

Only when the horse has found its rhythm in free tempo, moves fluently and is supple, accepts a light contact on the bit and lets the rider sit comfortably, can we begin the training of the ridden tempi. Starting from the free tempo, the rider will gradually slow down, with the result that the horse's outline becomes more elevated and the quarters engaged. At the other end of the scale, the trainer will start in a free tempo tölt, gradually increasing the speed and the horse should now stretch and its movements should cover more ground.

Problem: breaking into trot

This happens when horses react to half halts by becoming tighter and tighter, and the front elevation becomes too extreme, until the horse breaks into trot. Either the rider's combined aids failed to get through, or his rein aids were simply too crude. The trainer has to take his time during downward transitions

Breaking into trot: the horse reacts to the half halt by becoming tight and front elevation becomes too extreme. The horse isn't stretching because the trainer has either 'forgotten' to give with the reins, or he didn't create enough forward impulsion. The horse comes into negative flow, breaks into trot and then walk.

and, at the same time, has to try to extend the horse's outline to ensure the flow of movement continues instead of aiming for more elevation.

Problem: increasing the tempo
The most frequent fault when increasing the speed is that horses are suddenly rushed into it. Even if a horse copes with the sudden 'push', the rider will probably fail to guide it into a balanced stretch, it will roll, or strike off in canter. The other possibility is that it ignores the rein aids, stretches too far forward, leans on the bit and starts to go pacey. Some horses react to brisk driving aids by dropping their shoulders, raising their necks and speeding off, needless to say in a negative flow, in a pacey or canter-like action. This carries a high risk of injury.

Five-gaited horses, especially, lose their suppleness at high speed and react to half halts with an extended outline, often fighting the bit. Should this happen, the rider needs to take his time when applying half halts and to concentrate on achieving collection.

Problem: turns
Difficulty in riding bends and turns shows that the horse is not equally well trained on both reins. Most tölters can only tackle bends without

The rider is 'attacking' his horse with his sudden demand for speed. It comes into negative flow, drops its shoulder, raises its neck and bolts. Not only is it impossible for the rider to sit, but there is also a danger that the horse sustains overreach injuries.

rolling, when they are on the rein they normally have problems with when striking-off in canter. On the other rein they will roll in every corner. The only way to approach this problem is to go back and 'sort out' the horse's natural crookedness.

Canter

Footfalls, seat and tempo

Canter is a three-beat gait with six phases. The sequence in which legs leave the ground is as follows: left hindleg, right hind and left foreleg together, right foreleg followed by a moment of suspension (canter right), or right hindleg, left hind and right fore together, left foreleg followed by a moment of suspension (canter left).

Canter can be ridden in the basic seat, the relief seat or the forward seat. In addition to free tempo, Icelandic Horses are also ridden in working and medium canter.

Aids for canter

Starting with a half halt, the rider asks his horse to bend to the right or left, according to which leading leg is required, and assumes a swivel seat: inside leg on the girth, outside leg about a hand-span behind the girth, more weight on the inner seat bone (pelvis more engaged on this side and hip pushed slightly forward),

Gaits – Canter

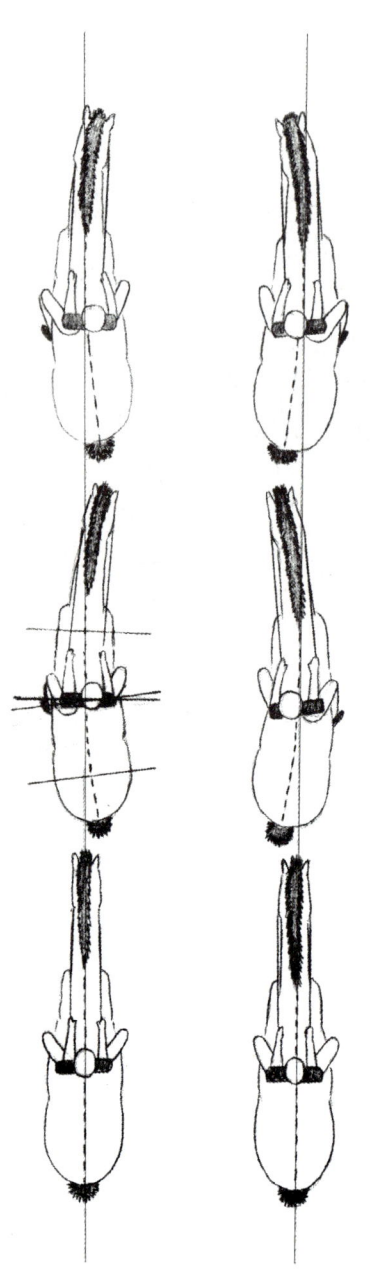

Before striking off in canter, the rider assumes a swivel seat and positions his horse accordingly (quarters in).

inner rein positions the horse, outside rein balances. The inside seat and leg aid encourages the horse to produce the first canter strike which is released by the rider with the inside rein. Every new canter step has to be 'produced' by the rider, who must keep applying the aids time and time again.

The trainer initially teaches the horse to strike off in canter on the lunge, using the fact that the horse is in a slight bend, and trains it to react to a signal of voice and whip. When ridden in the school, striking off is best practised from trot or tölt and to begin with, in a corner, later on the straight. Because a clear three-beat canter is more of a hindrance when concentrating on training of the special gaits, the trainer of an Icelandic Horse does not favour it much, at least in the beginning. It is therefore advisable for the rider to start by directing his horse into a four-beat canter first (almost simulating a rolling movement) and, when riding downward transitions, to try to get the hindlegs stepping instead of bouncing.

Natural predisposition and types
With Icelandic Horses, one can generally say that the more pace a horse has, the greater are its problems in producing a balanced canter, or in cantering around bends (see also self-carriage). The Icelandic Horse shows three main types of canter:

Gaits – Canter

Because the clear three-beat canter is more of a hindrance when training the special gaits, the trainer does not favour it much at first. Four-beat canter with downward transitions and trying to get the hindlegs stepping will help to balance a gaited horse.

Type: Strong three-beat canter

There is the type that naturally has a strong three-beat canter. This is almost always a four-gaiter. The hindquarters are lifted rather high off the ground and keep close together. This has very little in common with the running type movements of pace or tölt. The rider must try to sit well, applying seat aids, as when riding a big horse.

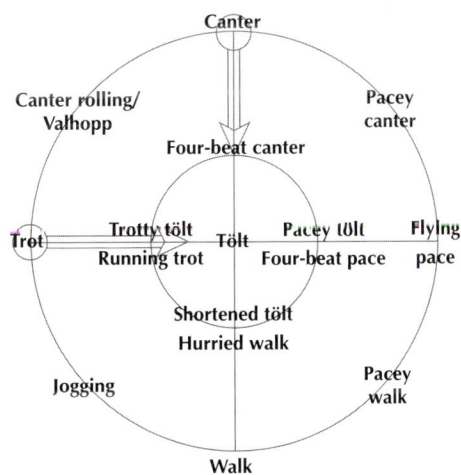

Gait: canter
Type: strong three-beat

90 Gaits – Canter

At first, when training these horses, canter work should be restricted to just letting them do their own thing. The rider's aim is to gradually close the gap between tölt and canter, until these types can be fluently moved in the direction of four-beat and therefore tölt (the croup is not moving up and down so much).

Type: Four-beat canter
The next type is exhibited by the running canter of the natural tölter, which is easily moved towards trot. These horses are very comfortable to ride because the quarters stay lower in canter and the shoulders are nicely raised. Through fast riding and changes of tempi out on hacks, or even better in company, they will increasingly stretch for the bit and, after thorough schooling, canter in

A horse that is forced into a certain outline cannot let movement flow through its body. Its back muscles are completely taut, thus making the canter so uncomfortable for the rider that even the best cannot sit properly.

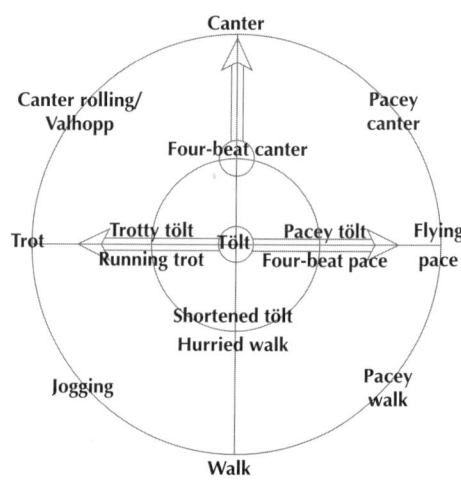

Gait: canter
Type: four-beat canter

the desired clear-beat with well engaged quarters.

Type: Pacey canter*

Finally, the Icelandic Horse rider can also encounter the pacey canter of a five-gaiter, a rather stiff and lateral movement. Horses can generally only be cantered in a straight line and give the rider a strong feeling of riding forward/downwards. They strike off badly and are immediately in negative flow (quarters high, back rigid, shoulders dropped) which very often leads to pace or disunited canter.

In disunited canter, the horse canters on one lead in front, for example canter right, and on the other lead with his hindlegs, in our example canter left. A horse that is in disunited canter is in negative flow.

With these horses, the trainer has to establish the other gaits firmly in positive flow before he begins canter training (see also tölt training of horses that are stiff towards pace).

Type Stiff canter with pace tendency
Unlike the type of horse that has a tendency towards pacey canter, these horses are able to maintain a relatively balanced canter. Riding bends in canter is possible, but such types find it increasingly difficult to

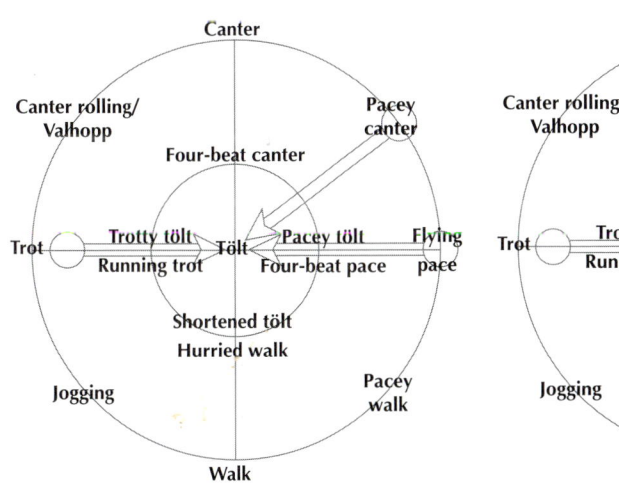

Gait: canter
Type: pacey canter

Gait: canter
Type: stiff canter with pace tendency

---

*Pacey canter is a four-beat canter, where the legs are put down in diagonal pairs – first with the front and then with the hindleg. The horse is in negative flow when showing pacey canter.

change outline or tempo. They break into a disunited canter when asked for a sudden increase in tempo, or, if the rider asks for a downward transition, they suddenly find themselves in stiff pace. However, if this type is sufficiently trained in tölt and trot and accepts fluent transitions into canter, this will automatically improve the canter as well, therefore rendering a special schooling programme for this type unnecessary.

Flying pace

Footfalls, seat and tempo

Pace is a two-beat gait with four phases. The horse moves laterally: left hindleg and left foreleg together and, after a moment of suspension, right hindleg and right foreleg together. Pace is only ridden on absolutely straight and even tracks, and exclusively at racing speed, as any other tempo would bring the horse into negative flow with high quarters, a rigid back and dropped shoulders. As with any gait that is performed at racing speed, the flying pace is, technically speaking, a four-beat. The hindlegs touch down a split second before the forelegs, thus making the flying pace, to be absolutely precise, a four-beat gait with eight phases. The high speed calls for adequate protection of the horses' legs. The rider employs a basic seat or a relief seat when riding flying pace.

Before attempting to ride flying pace, the rider has to ensure that his horse is well schooled in all the other gaits and can maintain positive flow with engaged quarters, supple back and raised shoulders at all times. It is also important that his horse is strong enough and in good physical and sound psychological condition before pace training starts. Typically, a rider has to invest two to three years in sound basic schooling before his horse can deliver good performance in flying pace, without the danger of lasting physical or mental damage.

Focus on flying pace
Riding flying pace is especially difficult, as the rider's aids, executed at high speed, have to be particularly skilful and effective. For that reason we shall divide this chapter into two parts. In the first, we will again separate flying pacers into types, in order to assess and plan their further schooling. In the second part, we

Riding flying pace is especially difficult as the rider's aids, executed at high speed, have to be particularly skilful and effective. Good flying pacers need to be in good physical and sound psychological condition. Most are real characters and well known to everybody on the 'scene'. For instance Fjölnir frá Kvíabekk who won the pace race (21.7seconds) and came second in five-gait at the European Championships in 1983 at Roderath with Thomas Ragnarsson; or Sigurboði frá Reykjum, ridden by Karlheinz Keßler, who came third in five-gait at the European Championships in 1977 at Skiveren (bottom).

94 Gaits – Flying pace

will concentrate on a close examination of pace riding at speed. This is because a stiff horse can actually supple up during a race and consequently needs to be checked like a balanced horse.

Flying pace: the types
Type: The pacer with strong four-beat

Just like the natural tölter, there are many horses that pace in a strong four-beat, with high self carriage and action, but generally they have difficulty in stretching out. Riding these horses too fast, or putting too much pressure on them at the start of their flying pace training, will only result in raised shoulders. The trainer

The so-called four-beat pacers are horses with high self-carriage and leg action and their pace is almost a clear four-beat.

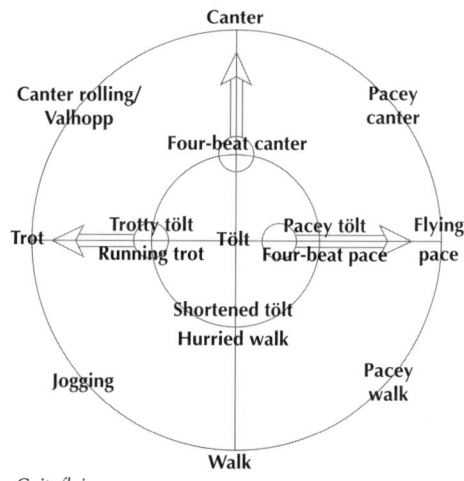

Gait: flying pace
Type: strong four-beat

Gaits – Flying pace

This type of pacer, with an extended and stretched outline, can really move fast as shown here by Byr and Nadine Beutler. How much you can achieve when horse and rider understand each other has been demonstrated by this pair again and again, for example when they took the German five-gait Champion title in 1991.

needs to take his time by not pressurising them and he should attempt the transition into pace (switching) from a more sedate tempo. Every now and then, the rider can let them stretch from a fast tölt into flying pace, riding in a relief seat, as these types can do with a little rounding of their backs. This kind of horse should be asked for flying pace over longer distances while the speed is gradually increased. For pace training the rider should select a flat, even track with firm ground. A slight downhill inclination is acceptable, but take care never to select an uphill track.

Type: The pacer with an extended and stretched outline

Such horses are best switched from gallop into flying pace by applying lots of pressure. The rider is actually increasing the speed of the gallop until the horse reaches flying pace speed. As they normally canter rather badly, these horses are usually quite relieved when they are allowed to change gait. That is why they often switch into pace by them-

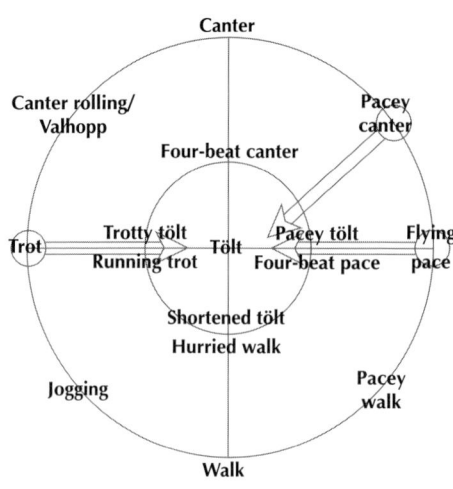

Gait: flying pace
Type: extended, stretched outline

well schooled in all other gaits before flying pace training can begin. They are best switched out of a sedate canter, using lots of pressure to get them into flying pace and, again, with pressure, encouraged to speed up. With these horses too, it is the lesser of two evils when they escape the high pressure by 'jumping upwards' (positive flow), instead of breaking into the two-beat and end up in Víxl (negative flow). This 'jumping upwards' is far easier to correct by the rider, by fine-tuning the applied pressure.

During training, the rider generally switches the horse into pace very firmly. If the horse skips when it goes into pace and becomes too high or too tight, the rider should allow it to stretch out again into a gallop and then switch back into pace. This 'game' has to be repeated patiently until a decent speed in pace is achieved and the rider is able to decrease or increase the tempo fluently without ending up in negative flow. Only when this is established should the rider attempt to try for higher speed, or to require a reasonably high standard to be maintained.

These horses need plenty of time before they become really fast. If the rider experiences problems, for instance if the horse breaks gait a lot or can't change into an easy four-beat, then this is a sign that either the suppling exercises haven't been successful, or the basic schooling in other gaits is not advanced enough.

selves as soon as strong driving aids during gallop are stopped. However, they do have a tendency to quickly topple into negative flow, resulting in Víxl. For this reason, they should not be ridden in pace over long distances. When the rider asks for flying pace, he should gradually increase the speed and prevent his horse from getting too low. He should also ride rather provocatively and accept the odd skip or break into the four-beat. These horses should always be slowed with lots of pressure to avoid them becoming low in front or going into Víxl. That is why the basic seat is best.

Type: The stiff horse

In this group, we find the stiff five-gaiter, a horse that has to be very

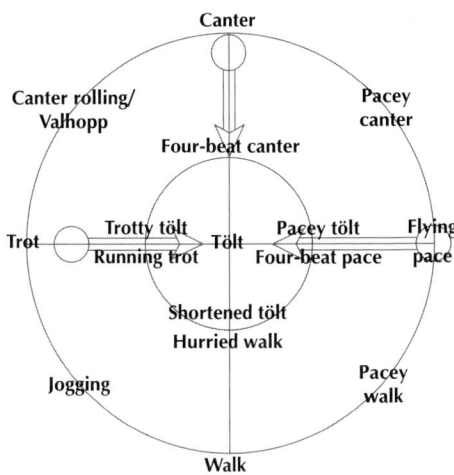

Gait: flying pace
Type: the stiff type

It is equally important for the stiff pacer to accept being checked firmly, reacting with collection and not by tensing up. Forcing these horses too abruptly, with a rigid hand pulling the reins upwards, will all too easily leave them in negative flow. It is, however, possible that the horse becomes loose and supple during the flying pace and ends the race in positive flow and can be checked with ease. The rider should preferably select slight uphill tracks with softish ground. A slightly uneven surface can be beneficial, as it makes the horse concentrate. Tracks where the horse will accept driving aids are best, which means that pacing at full speed along a downhill path, perhaps even towards home, is to be avoided.

When the will to race is missing
Finally, there are flying pacers who don't wish to go forward, because nobody has actually taught them how to race. They will benefit from being ridden in a group, or from being asked to pace on the way home. The trainer has to try to instil a joy of running into these horses, either by taking them as a hand horse, or letting them gallop flat out on tracks, where he will later train flying pace. Lazy horses shouldn't be ridden much in flying pace, but the trainer should concentrate on riding the other gaits in a more active tempo.

Here is one central idea for all trainers: if other gaits suffer when training flying pace, then either your horse has not been properly prepared, or the pace training is wrong.

Flying pace – riding at speed
Flying pace can be divided into three phases: switching, riding flying pace and checking.

We will describe the phases in a racing situation.

Switching to flying pace
The horse can best perform a clean transition into flying pace when it is switched from a flat out gallop. This is supported by the fact that you will only get high marks for style during competitions when flying pace is developed from gallop. Strictly speaking, this switching (the transition from gallop to flying pace) is

just a variation of a half halt, as the rider drives his horse from a gallop into his hands, or just uses the momentum of the gallop and immediately gives again and lets the horse stretch. Depending on how sensitively the horse reacts, this aid might need to be applied several times.

Faults when switching
The horse is still in positive flow but the aids for the switch only result in slowing down the gallop and making the horse tighter. These horses can sometimes almost skip on the spot and are unable to find the lateral. To correct this, the rider has to gallop forward again in order to regain a stretched outline. When switching the next time, emphasis should be on releasing the reins rather than the driving aids. Now give up the constant rein contact and try to switch by using one short and vigorous signal alone.

The horse is in a pacey canter – negative flow. Although it is possible to switch with forceful rein aids, the neck will come up too high and the horse will break into disunited canter after a few meters. It may even react to the aid to 'switch' by immediately going into a disunited canter. Very skilful riders might be able to 'save' these horses at the point of switching, if they can raise the dropped shoulders of a pacey canter

Flying pace is best achieved when switching from a flat out gallop. Strictly speaking, this transition is a variation of a half halt, as the rider drives his horse from gallop into his hands and immediately gives again and lets it stretch into pace.

by sensitively riding forward into pace. However, this rescue manoeuvre is only recommended for competitions, as the question of 'will it or won't it switch' is a poker game. During training, we should concentrate on a clean correction: speed up out of pacey canter until the horse is in positive flow. The next attempt to switch should be by driving vigorously, but at the same time being extremely sensitive with the rein aids, making sure the horse's neck doesn't come up.

Switching a horse from disunited canter is physically almost impossible if one looks closely at the footfalls. Very experienced flying pace riders are able, by applying strong half halts, or by zigzagging across the track, to get the horse into Víxl, then switching and carrying on pacing. Some horses prove so rigid and tense in disunited canter that they have to be checked right back almost to a standstill to encourage Víxl. Other horses manage this without problems, sometimes without their over-excited riders even noticing. However, it has to be said that the majority of flying pacers do get rather distressed in disunited canter, and as soon as a half halt is applied, they snatch the bit and bolt. Therefore, in training, switching out of disunited canter should be discouraged. The less often a horse experiences crude rein aids by trying to force it to switch, the more relaxed the horse will become in disunited canter. If it is generally checked back in a subtle manner and asked for correct strike-off, then the rider can probably risk the odd

100 Gaits – Flying pace

In flying pace, the rider has to watch that his horse remains in positive flow. The horse's body should always have an uphill feel and the pace should be close to a four-beat.

rescue manoeuvre in a race without a panic reaction from his horse. When it becomes necessary during a competition for the rider to force Víxl, then he should never follow this with forceful aids.

A horse that often exhibits disunited canter is probably still too tense in its whole body to strike off correctly. The more naturally balanced a horse is in canter and the better it is schooled in this gait, the less likely is the danger that it will break into disunited canter. Supple, well-trained horses that strike off accidentally in disunited canter do generally correct themselves after a few meters.

Aids when riding flying pace

The most important thing is for the rider to monitor that his horse is still in positive flow. The horse's body should constantly feel like it is going slightly uphill and the flying pace should always be close to a four-beat.

Faults when riding flying pace

A horse that is too close to four-beat when pacing, or is too high in its outline and has a tendency to skip or break into racing tölt, has to be stretched more by the rider. Such horses should be ridden calmly without requesting sudden bursts of speed. It is better to ride on longer tracks and to give them the opportunity to develop speed out of a stretched position.

A horse might perform flying pace in an extremely stretched outline, raise the quarters, drop the shoulders (negative flow) and break gait after a few meters. Here the rider has to work on improving the horse's sensitivity to half halts when performing flying pace. He needs to be able to collect the horse and shorten its outline before it gets into negative flow. Sudden, forceful checking is very bad for this type of horse. However, even horses like these can be corrected when it matters, for example during competitions. The rider should ride forward with all his might, hoping that the horse can cope with this 'attack'. This should only be used as an emergency measure in exceptional cases, because many horses will 'lose it' during the attempt, and repeatedly bad experiences will turn them into unreliable mounts under race conditions.

Checking from flying pace

The rider should never allow the horse to end a flying pace session in gallop or, even worse, in disunited canter. The correct way to finish is to apply half halts patiently at the end of the racetrack and to take time to achieve some collection, especially when training the young horse.

Faults when checking the horse

If a horse has a tendency to skip (positive flow) when being checked, this normally indicates that the rider has to concentrate more on sensitive rein aids in order to maintain a stretched outline. Horses that become rather low in front and break into a two-beat (negative flow) need to be brought back gradually onto their haunches without risking a high head carriage (this will happen when only the reins are used to stop the movement). This would result in negative flow and lead to Víxl.

Competition Riding

Competition riding is a subject that a book like this cannot do justice to. Rather than leaving it out completely, we will give you some basic ideas.

Purpose of competitions

Competitions offer a good opportunity to asses the rider's level of training, the horse's progress and, most importantly, to judge the performance of the horse/rider team. By receiving marks, comments from the judges, or from judges' forms, the rider gets an evaluation of his

Competitions offer a good opportunity to assess one's own level of training as well as the horse's progress. The most important thing in a competition should be the harmony between horse and rider.

accomplishment and, if he is lucky, advice on how to improve further.

Shows are also useful for a rider to demonstrate how well he is getting on with his horse in unfamiliar surroundings. He can exchange experiences with like-minded people, socialise and compete with others. But ultimately, competitions are about winning or, at least, being up there in the places.

Evaluating performance realistically

To avoid disappointment, it is immensely important that a rider has learned to rate himself and his horse's performance realistically. Instructors, judges, or other competition riders can help with this. One thing a rider has to be aware of is the possibility that his horse will not perform as well at the show as it works at home, and he must therefore choose his classes with care. Basic rules are: 'favour the easier classes and leave the more difficult ones for later' and: 'better enter one class too few than one too many'. It is not only hopes that can be shattered when a rider is overconfident in the choice of tests. In the worst scenario, it can endanger the whole training when, for instance, a nervous five-gaiter refuses to trot in the warm-up area and an irritable rider reacts by using methods the horse cannot understand. A sensible animal will lose faith in its trainer and may stop trotting altogether, even at home.

Shows represent quite an extreme situation for both humans and animals alike, and the horse needs to be able to look to a person for reassurance. This person should be able to devote plenty of time to the horse and, ideally, should be the rider himself. He should provide the best accommodation he can afford and feed his horse a little more at shows (in moderation), just to pamper it a bit. Horses that are happy and content are more likely to concentrate and co-operate than those that aren't.

Warming up

During the warming up sessions, or even better a day before the first test, the rider should introduce his horse to the track where the class will be held. Planning the time for riding-in is especially important on competition day (get a timetable and starting list to help you with this), as well as finding the ideal place on the show ground. For example; a rather top heavy five-gaiter is best not warmed up in the dressage arena, where the deep ground will bring it even more onto the forehand. The rider has to be absolutely sure of what situation, ground conditions and sort of surroundings his horse prefers in order to relax (see Gaits). It is therefore vital to take note of any advantage the show ground might offer, as proper warming up areas are usually rare.

The rider is strongly advised not to practise any exercises that exceed the standard of the actual test. Any failure will put him and his horse off and valuable time will be wasted. It is also unwise to use the warming up area to try to teach the horse something that has been 'forgotten' at home. Another point to watch out for is not to overdo the riding-in. This is often seen when exercises go wrong in the warming up session and the rider perseveres. Never forget that the most important issue in a competition is be the harmony between horse and rider and not the laboured execution of a test.

After the competition

The rider should take time to attend to his horse properly after a competition. If the performance was not as he had hoped for, he should just calm down and under no circumstances go back to the warm up area and resume practising, or even attempt to punish his horse. Don't lose faith in your horse; every competition is just one little step on the long road to perfection. After all, competitions and shows are the only occasions where horse and rider can gain experience and become familiar with a competitive situation and it is to be expected that things will sometimes go wrong.

Saddlery and Tack

The Saddle

Basically, a saddle should be built in such a way that its deepest point is right in the middle of the seat. The centre of the saddle should always be placed over the horse's centre of gravity, as this is fundamental in achieving a combined balance of horse and rider.

Requirements of the saddle

One fundamental requirement is that the saddle should lie on the horse without causing pressure sores. The more weight a saddle is designed to bear, the bigger the supporting surface on the horse's back should be. This is why you will find that endurance or trekking saddles have longer panels to distribute the weight of the rider and any saddlebags over a larger area. Problems can occur when the horse has a rather short back, as these saddles and the longer panels will sit right over the kidney area, which could lead to problems when riding turns. For pure competition riding, these

Saddlery and tack 105

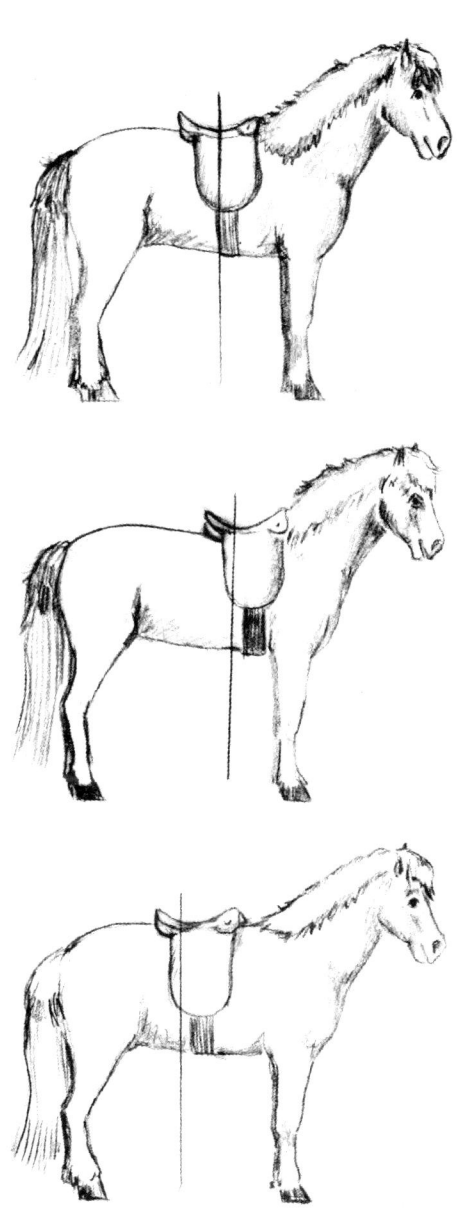

Top: saddle is over the centre of gravity
Centre: too far forward
Bottom: too far back

longer panels offer no benefits whatsoever.

When choosing a saddle, it is wise to look for a narrow seat. Broad saddles tend to pull the rider's legs apart at the point of the hip, which, especially on a narrow horse, gives the rider little chance to bring his legs onto the horse.

When riding an Icelandic Horse, the riding position is rather different, with a more extended leg and longer stirrups. The chosen saddle should therefore have flaps that are cut straight rather than cut forward (as on a more conventional type of saddle). It is also beneficial to look for a longer flap to avoid the unpleasant problem suffered by many taller riders of getting the tops of their riding boots caught under the saddle flap.

Problems with the height of the pommel are virtually unheard of, as Icelandic Horses rarely have very pronounced withers. Their rather low withers are also responsible for the fact that a saddle on an Icelandic Horse will seldom slip backwards. However, there can be problems with the width of the gullet. When a saddle is too narrow at this point, it will not lie low enough in front and any amount of girth tightening will not fix the saddle sufficiently and the saddle will slip forward. The same can happen if the rider has selected a gullet that is too wide, as the saddle will not find any hold. Nowadays, many saddles come with one girth strap placed further forward, in order to assist in fixing the saddle properly.

If this is not sufficient, the cross-country and leisure rider can always rely on a crupper. This is quite easy to use and generally serves its purpose well. It has to be said, however, that sensitive horses may not go so well with a crupper attached to the saddle. This is the reason for the development of the front girth, aimed particularly at the competition rider, as a means of fixing the saddle without the negative attributes of a crupper.

Problem: unsuitable saddles
A rider who wants to sit close to the horse's movements, align his weight with the horse's centre of gravity and get through with his pelvic aids may run into great problems when choosing a saddle that was specially developed for Icelandic Horses. Riders of pacey tölters or other tense horses can only avoid the effect of the strong lateral movement by bracing themselves against the stirrups and sitting further and further back. Saddles were therefore built with the deepest point located towards the rear of the seat. This altered the centre of gravity, by placing it further back. This allowed the rider to push his legs forward and grip with the upper thighs. In this position, the rider's seat couldn't go with the rhythm, the hips tilted backwards and the shoulders hunched. Some saddles even sported so-called 'upper thigh stops' and a few saddlers tried to give helplessly swaying legs some support by placing special 'rear thigh supports' on the sweat flaps. On top of all that, these saddles were often rather insecure as the weight of the rider was in the latter third of the seat, thus lifting the front arch over the horse's withers and the whole saddle began to slip forward.

Placing the saddle further back
Icelandic Horses are normally saddled much further back than are other breeds, simply because they have a different centre of gravity. However, saddling even further back behind the horse's centre of gravity, as done by many a rider who thought he could thereby force the quarters down, should be rejected. The hindquarters can only be brought down by means of gymnastic exercises, not by a saddle that places increasing pressure on the horse's kidneys. Jarring, as indeed any use of force, will only tense the quarters and destroy the natural flow of movement through the body. The horse's shoulders will stay low and any form of collection will be impossible.

This extreme saddle position will also cause the horse problems when turning and can result in the lumbar vertebrae becoming increasingly immobile and, in the extreme, even to fuse. It should be remembered that the rider actually inflicts pain on his horse when the end of the panels dig into the horse's kidneys, especially the longer panels of endurance saddles.

Bits

Opinions differ when it comes to bits. Shape, material and size have become one of the most important subjects for some riders. We believe bits are simply a personal choice and, in our opinion, a simple, single jointed snaffle is totally adequate for schooling purposes. This bit (about 12 cm in width and 20 mm in diameter) can be used safely for the duration of basic training. However, the rider/trainer should use the bit that suits his particular horse best.

It is far more important to work diligently on any faults or shortcomings that show up during the horse's training, rather than simply changing the bit. Experience shows that the effect of a new bit will wear off quite quickly if the rider does not restructure the training of his horse and correct possible faults at the same time.

The Icelandic bit

The Icelandic bit is a single jointed curb bit that works extremely well when riding finely and thoroughly schooled horses on a long, straight track. Depending on what you do with the curb chain, it is possible to employ the Icelandic bit in two very

The most frequent dilemma when using the Icelandic bit incorrectly: when the horse's natural crookedness has not been dealt with properly and the horse tightens laterally. The cheek engaged strongly on one side is clearly visible.

different ways. When the curb chain is fitted loosely, or not used at all, the bit will work like a normal snaffle and the rider should maintain equal rein contact. If the curb chain is fitted normally, the bit will now act with a lever action and is best used for signal riding. For example, when switching into flying pace the rider will take the reins up for a brief moment (a sort of gentle tugging aid) and immediately let the horse stretch again. When the Icelandic bit has been used incorrectly, the most frequently seen dilemma is lateral tightening on one side of the horse. The underlying problem is the natural crookedness of the horse, which has not been dealt with properly

108 Saddlery and tack

The Icelandic bit is a single jointed curb bit that works extremely well when riding finely and thoroughly schooled horses on a long, straight track.

during the warming up session. It is quite visible; one cheek is strongly engaged, the other hangs loose, and the rider has little or no rein contact on the latter side. In order to correct this, the curb chain should be fitted loosely or taken away altogether (better still, change to a snaffle) and the natural crookedness should be dealt with first.

Protective Accessories

During a flying pace race, or when a high-speed tölt is required, the rider should consider giving his horse's legs some special protection.

Overreach injuries are quite common when riding bends during pace or tölt. They are the consequence of a tense horse being rushed into a corner and the flow of movement losing its fluency and harmony. This usually leads to the diagonal hindleg crashing, at that particular moment, into the only supporting foreleg. The injuries a horse can sustain are either the direct result of tension, or because the horse is simply not up to the job. Perhaps the rider selected an unsuitable riding surface and the horse tensed up in order to grip better, or the horse's training was just not advanced enough to perform the desired speed in complete balance.

Preventative leg protection is always advisable, as horses will quickly lose confidence after having hurt themselves badly. They might not dare to use their hindlegs actively for quite some time and may try to muddle through by skipping for a while.

For horses that are likely to injure themselves in the splint, cannon bone area, or the fetlock, brushing boots offer the best protection. The heel is best protected with overreach boots.

Fitted heel boots and quarter boots have proved successful as 'shoe-savers' (when the horse's hind-foot steps onto the back of the front shoe) as the hind shoe then virtually slides over the protruding front shoe.

NEED INFORMATION

WE CAN HELP!

- information on breeders and sellers
- information on export services
- information about transport
- information on sales shows and services
- information about bloodlines and breeding marks
- information about Icelandic horses worldwide
- Promotional materials
    - brochures
    - videos
    - books

WHATEVER YOU NEED TO KNOW, WE WILL TRY TO FIND OUT.

FÉLAG HROSSABÆNDA

Please contact:
Horsebreeders Association
c/o Hulda G. Geirsdóttir
Bændahöllinni v/Hagatorg
107 Reykjavík, Iceland
Phone: +354 563 0300
Fax: +354 562 5211
e-mail: f.hrb@bi.bondi.is

Make your dream come true!
ADVENTURE TOURS ON HORSEBACK IN ICELAND

ISHESTAR offers a wide range of tours. Let Iceland be your next destination for adventure and fall in love with our unique horses.

1 - 6 day tours: ❖

Our popular day tours in which we explore the **Reykjavík** vicinity will give you a whole new view of Iceland's capital. We offer farm house accommodation and riding tours close to **Mt. Hekla**. We also offer horse tours to the well-known hot spring area **Geysir** and to **Gullfoss** waterfalls.

Highland tours: ❖

Riding on historical horse routes alongside a herd of free-running horses – the experience of a lifetime! On our **Kjölur** and **Sprengisandur** tours we follow in the footsteps of Icelanders who in centuries past travelled on horseback through the interior. Observe bubbling mud springs and craters in the North and herds of reindeer in the East. Enjoy **tölt** for long stretches on the beaches of the **Snæfellsnes peninsula**, or the multi-coloured mountains of the **Landmannalaugar** area.

Mountain cabins offer sleeping-bag accommodation. Luggage is transported by a kitchen van and our cook prepares warm meals each evening. Later, join in the singing and hear stories of horsemen and outlaws, as well as other tales from this fascinating country.

Find your dream-tour with us!

ÍS HESTAR — *The leaders for over 15 years.*

PLEASE CONTACT US FOR FURTHER DETAILS.
FOR INFORMATION PHONE (+354) 565 3044 OR FAX (+354) 565 2113
E-MAIL: INFO@ISHESTAR.IS, WEBSITE: WWW.ISHESTAR.IS

RICHARD HINRICHS

Schooling Horses in-Hand

Means of suppling-up and collection.

Anyone wishing to train horses to a high level requires experience in dealing with horses as well as specialised knowledge concerning the training system and suitable methods. For centuries schooling in-hand has been commonly acknowledged as a highly effective method.
It is an excellent way of supporting and complementing the work under the rider.
Richard Hinrichs, a well-known expert, demonstrates the classical training of horses and pupils. Trust, obedience and balance develop quite naturally when training is carefully and gradually developed in a way which is adapted to suit the horse.

- Auxiliary aids and their application
- Suppling-up on the lunge
- Shoulder-in and half-pass
- Pirouette, piaffe and passage
- Long reining
- Airs above the ground

Video

Address for orders:
Kosmos Verlags-GmbH & Co.
Foreign Rights Department
Pfizerstr. 5 – 7
D -70184 Stuttgart
Fax: ++49/711/ 2191 329

Bibliographical data:
ISBN: 3-440-07921-X
Film duration: approx. 45 minutes
DM: 42,93 excl. VAT + freight
Reduced prices for traders

kosmos

Books • Videos • CDs • Calendars

If you have enjoyed reading this book and you would like to give one to a friend or you just want to order more, please contact the publisher direct, or e-mail me, or have a look at my webpage:

www.dream-teams.com

DREAM TEAM
Birgit Michaux
Home Farm
Bicester, Poundon
OX26 0AY
England

e-mail: bnonnenprediger@hotmail.com